CHOICES

ELEMENTARY WORKBOOK
with Audio CD

T0346221

ROD FRICKER

CONTENTS

A Get Ready

1 Complete the words and match them with the numbers.

1	e _i_ g _h_ t	_c_	**a**	33
2	_ _ _ _ n _ y	___	**b**	15
3	_ h _ _ t _ - t _ _ e _	___	**c**	8
4	_ _ r _	___	**d**	12
5	_ _ f _ _ - _ _ v _	___	**e**	14
6	_ _ _ f _ _ e _	___	**f**	20
7	_ _ u _ t _ _ _ _	___	**g**	55
8	_ _ _ r _ _ _ - _ _ n _	___	**h**	0
9	_ w _ _ v _	___	**i**	49

2 Complete the sentences with the correct form of the verb *be*.

1 Where ___*are*___ you from?
2 _____ he a teacher?
3 We _____ from Italy. We're from France.
4 She _____ a student. She's a teacher.
5 I _____ fifteen. I'm sixteen.
6 _____ you from Argentina? Yes, I _____ .
7 _____ she seventeen? No, she _____ .
8 _____ I in your class? Yes, you _____ .

3 Choose the correct words to complete the sentences.

1 How old are ⟨you⟩/your?
2 What's *you/your* name?
3 Who's *we're/our* teacher?
4 *She's/ Her* name is Claudia.
5 What's *he's/his* address?
6 *We're/Our* from Spain.
7 *I'm/My* name is Tom.
8 *She/Her* is the school secretary.
9 *He's/His* in my class.
10 *They're/Their* eighteen.

4 Complete the text with the words below. There is one extra word.

her   he's   his   I'm   ~~my~~   our   she   we

Hi. [1] ___*My*___ name's Debbie. [2] _____ from Australia. This my friend. [3] _____ name is Lisa. [4] _____ is in my class at school. [5] _____ French teacher's name is Jean-Paul. [6] _____ like him. [7] _____ very nice.

5 Match the questions with the correct answers.

1 Are you a student? ___*i*___
2 What's your name? ___
3 Can you spell your name, please? ___
4 Where are you from? ___
5 How old are you? ___
6 What's your address? ___
7 What's your phone number? ___
8 Who is your teacher? ___
9 Is he nice? ___

a It's 078463295.
b Yes, he is.
c Melanie
d I'm sixteen.
e M-E-L-A-N-I-E
f Mr Thomas.
g 38, Market Street, Coventry.
h I'm from England.
i Yes, I am.

6 Complete the names of the countries.

1 B r _i_ t _a_ _i_ n
2 _ r g _ n t _ n _
3 S p _ _ _ n
4 C z _ _ c h R _ p _ b l _ c
5 R _ m _ n _ _ _
6 _ _ _ s t r _ l _ _
7 B _ l g _ r _ _ _
8 H _ n g _ r y
9 _ k r _ _ _ n _
10 B r _ z _ l

7 Write about the people who are speaking.

1

> Hi, my name's Cathy. I'm from New York.

Her name's Cathy. She's from New York.

2

> My name's Tom. I'm from Prague.

_____

_____

3

> Our names are Josie and Maria. We're from Sao Paolo.

_____

_____

4

> My name's Andrea. I'm a student. I'm seventeen years old.

_____

_____

5

> My name's Ed. I'm thirty-four years old. I'm a teacher.

_____

_____

6

> Our name's are Erika and Suzi. We're students. We're sixteen years old.

_____

_____

8 Look at the information and sentences about Silvio. Write similar information about Dana.

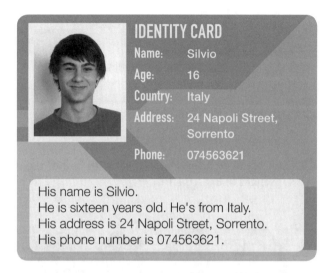

IDENTITY CARD

Name: Silvio
Age: 16
Country: Italy
Address: 24 Napoli Street, Sorrento
Phone: 074563621

His name is Silvio.
He is sixteen years old. He's from Italy.
His address is 24 Napoli Street, Sorrento.
His phone number is 074563621.

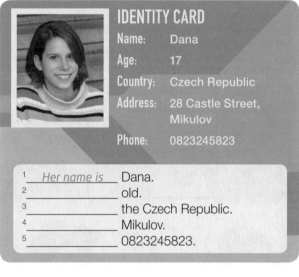

IDENTITY CARD

Name: Dana
Age: 17
Country: Czech Republic
Address: 28 Castle Street, Mikulov
Phone: 0823245823

1 _Her name is_ Dana.
2 _____ old.
3 _____ the Czech Republic.
4 _____ Mikulov.
5 _____ 0823245823.

9 Write about your personal information.

_____

_____

_____

_____

B Get Ready

1a Complete the sentences with the correct words. You can see the first letter of each word.

1 W*ork*_____ in groups of four.
2 D_____ Exercise 5 for homework.
3 U_____ a dictionary.
4 C_____ the table in your books.
5 R_____ the text.
6 A_____ and a_____ the questions with your partner.
7 O_____ your books on page 15.

1b Look at the pictures. Match them with four of the sentences in Exercise 1a.

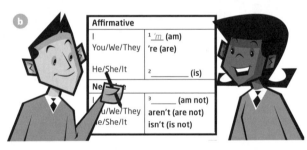

Affirmative

I	¹ _'m_ (am)
You/We/They	're (are)
He/She/It	² _____ (is)

Ne____

I	
u/We/They	aren't (are not)
e/She/It	isn't (is not)
	³ _____ (am not)

Countries of the world

a _Work in groups of four._
b _____
c _____
d _____

2 Choose the correct words to complete the sentences.

1 *Listen to/Read* two people talking.
2 *Look at/Watch* the photo in your book.
3 *Watch/Look* the DVD.
4 *Match/Complete* the questions with the answers.
5 *Tell/Speak* English.
6 *Ask/Answer* your partner some questions.
7 *Tell/Speak* me the answer.
8 *Ask/Answer* your partner's questions.

3 Make negative sentences using the verbs below.

~~speak~~ do look at open tell use watch write

1 _Don't speak_ Italian in English classes.
2 _____ the DVD
3 _____ your books.
4 _____ your partner the answer.
5 _____ Exercise 4.
6 _____ your mobile phone in the classroom.
7 _____ the answers.
8 _____ in your Students' Book.

4 Correct the sentences.

1 Not speak in class.
   Don't speak in class.
2 Working in pairs.
   _____
3 Don't to use a mobile phone in class.
   _____
4 You can repeat that, please?
   _____
5 Do complete the table.
   _____
6 No write your name.
   _____
7 Can you again play the CD, please?
   _____

C Get Ready

1 Match the beginnings (1-5) with the endings (a-e).

1 Speak _e_
2 Count ___
3 Say ___
4 Spell ___
5 Tell ___

a the time in German.
b your name in Italian.
c to twenty in Spanish.
d the alphabet in Russian.
e French.

2 Choose the correct answers to the questions.

1 I can _b_ tennis
  a ride   b play   c dance
2 Can you ___ a bicycle?
  a write   b play   c ride
3 My dad can't ___ music from the internet.
  a download   b draw   c upload
4 Can your friend ___ a musical instrument.
  a sing   b play   c dance
5 Luke can ___ great stories.
  a paint   b draw   c write
6 Lucy always ___ her holiday photos onto her website.
  a draws   b uploads   c plays

3 Look at the table. Write sentences with *can* and *can't*.

	can	can't
1 Me	ski	ride a bike
2 Peter	sing	play a musical instrument
3 My brother	draw, paint	-
4 Tom	use a computer	find information on the internet
5 Anna	dance	sing
6 My parents	speak French, speak German	

1 *I can ski but I can't ride a bike.*
2 _____
3 _____
4 _____
5 _____
6 _____

4 Write short replies.

1 A: Can you count to a hundred in German?
   B: ✗ _No, I can't._
2 A: Can Lisa ski?
   B: ✓ _____
3 A: Can you and your friend sing?
   B: ✗ _____
4 A: Can they swim?
   B: ✓ _____
5 A: Can your dad draw?
   B: ✗ _____
6 A: Can you speak Italian?
   B: ✗ _____

D Get Ready

1 Label the pictures.

1 b*ag*_____ **2** b_____

3 e_____ **4** g_____

5 m_____ **6** t_____
   p_____   r_____

7 s_____ **8** T-s_____

2 Complete the colours.

1 Red and ____*white*____ makes ____*pink*____ .
2 Blue and y_____ makes g_____ .
3 B_____ and white makes g_____ .
4 Red and y_____ makes o_____ .
5 Red and b_____ makes p_____ .

3 Match the adjectives with the pictures.

big cheap expensive new ~~old~~ small

1 ____*old*____ **2** _____

3 _____ **4** _____

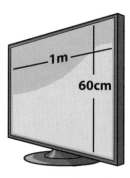 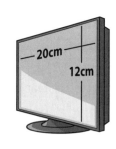

5 _____ **6** _____

4 Choose the correct words to complete the sentences.

1 *This is/These are* my books.
2 *That is/Those are* your class.
3 *Is that/Are those* my coursebook?
4 *Is this/Are these* our pens?
5 *This isn't/These aren't* his shoes.
6 *That isn't/Those aren't* her pictures.
7 *That is/Those are* his dictionary.
8 *This is/These are* their photos.

5 Write sentences with *this, that, these* and *those*.

1 ☞X my book
   This is my book.

2 ☞   x his shoes
   _____

3 ☞   x her MP3 player
   _____

4 ☞X our books
   _____

5 ☞X their photos
   _____

6 ☞   x my scarf
   _____

6 Choose the correct words to complete the sentences.

1 These are _b_ books.
   a Toms   **b** Tom's   **c** Toms'

2 Is this ___ phone?
   a Bill's   **b** Bills'   **c** Bills

3 That's our ___ car.
   a teachers   **b** teacher's   **c** teachers'

4 These are my ___ CDs.
   a parents'   **b** parents   **c** parent's

5 Is that ___ house?
   a Frances   **b** France's   **c** Frances's

6 What's your ___ address?
   a friends'   **b** friends   **c** friend's

7 I don't know my ___ phone number.
   a grandparents   **b** grandparent's   **c** grandparents'

7 Complete the sentences with two of the words in capitals.

1 ~~PARENTS~~ ~~PARENTS'~~ PARENT'S
   a My ___*parents*___ are teachers.
   b My ___*parents'*___ car is red.

2 FRIENDS FRIEND'S FRIENDS'
   a My _____ name is John.
   b Your _____ names are Steven and Lisa.

3 GRANDPARENTS GRANDPARENT'S GRANDPARENTS'
   a My _____ address is 21 London Road, Dartford.
   b My _____ aren't from Britain.

4 TEACHERS TEACHER'S TEACHERS'
   a Our _____ are very nice.
   b This is the _____ room.

5 BROTHERS BROTHER'S BROTHERS'
   a How many _____ have you got?
   b My _____ new phone is really good.

8 Complete the sentences with the correct possessive pronoun.

1 This is my bag.
   This bag is ____*mine.*____

2 Is this his coat?
   Is this coat _____ ?

3 That's their car.
   That car is _____ .

4 Are these her photos?
   Are these photos _____ ?

5 These are your books.
   These books are _____ .

6 Those are our CDs.
   Those CDs are _____ .

9 Complete the dialogues with the correct possessive adjective or possessive pronoun.

my ~~your~~ mine yours

A: Could I use [1]____*your*____ mobile phone, please?
B: Yes, of course. Here you are. Where's [2]_____ ?
A: [3]_____ dad's got it. It's in his car. Er …
B: Yes? What's wrong?
A: I can't use this phone. [4]_____ isn't very new and is easy to use. Can you help me?
B: Of course.

his her his hers

A: I can see your dad. Is that [5]_____ car?
B: No. [6]_____ is old.
A: Is it your mum's car?
B: No, [7]_____ is red.
A: My mum's car is blue but [8]_____ favourite colour is red.

our their ours theirs

A: Anna and I play the guitar but these guitars aren't [9]_____ .
B: Where are your guitars?
A: [10]_____ guitars are at Anna's house. These are Tom and Simon's guitars.
B: Are these CDs [11]_____ ?
A: Yes, they are, well, they're Tom's.
B: Are Tom and Simon brothers?
A: Yes. [12]_____ dad plays the guitar, too.

E Get Ready

1 Complete the table with the correct words.

Family members

Boys/Men	Girls/Women
1 _father_	mother
2 _____	mum
3 husband	_____
4 _____	sister
5 grandfather	_____
6 son	_____
7 grandson	_____

2 Complete the words.

Eyes:
1 b _l u e_
2 b _ _ _ _ _
3 g _ _ _ _ _
4 g _ _ _ _

Hair:
5 l _ _ _ _
6 s _ _ r _
7 b _ _ n _
8 f _ _ _ _

Appearance:
9 t _ _ _ _
10 s _ _ _ _
11 o _ _ _ _ w _ _ _ _ _ _
12 s _ _ r _

3 Complete the sentences with the correct form of *have/has got.*

1 I / blue eyes
   I've got blue eyes.

2 Mark / long hair
   _____

3 Julie / a sister
   _____

4 My parents / a red car
   _____

5 We / a nice English teacher
   _____

6 They / red hair
   _____

4 Complete the sentences with the negative (–) and positive (+) forms of *have got.*

1 Tom (–) red hair. He (+) fair hair.
   Tom hasn't got red hair. He's got fair hair.

2 My parents (–) a new car. They (+) and old car.
   _____

3 Our English teacher (–) a new bag. He (+) an old bag.
   _____

4 My friends (–) CDs.They (+) MP3 players.
   _____

5 I (–) a sister. I (+) a brother.
   _____

6 You (–) English homework. You (+) French homework
   _____

5 Write questions and short answers.

1 **A:** your mum / red hair?
   B: ✓
   A: *Has your mum got red hair?*
   B: *Yes, she has.*

2 **A:** your friends / big families?
   B: ✗
   A: _____
   B: _____

3 **A:** your parents / grey hair?
   B: ✓
   A: _____
   B: _____

4 **A:** you / a sister?
   B: ✓
   A: _____
   B: _____

5 **A:** you / green eyes?
   B: ✗
   A: _____
   B: _____

6 **A:** I / a nice smile?
   B: ✓
   A: _____
   B: _____

6 Complete the days of the week and put them in the correct order.

M*onday*
F_____
Sa_____
Su_____
Th_____
Tu_____
W_____

1 *Monday*
2 _____
3 _____
4 _____
5 _____
6 _____
7 _____

7 Complete the conversation with the words below.

are   do   for   ~~got~~ (x 2)   has
have   is   tall   write

Teacher: Emily, tell me about one person from your family.

Emily: I have ¹_____*got*_____ one sister. Her name is Natalie. She is ²_____ and she ³_____ got dark hair. She ⁴_____ attractive and she has ⁵_____ a nice smile. Natalie and I ⁶_____ got brown eyes and we ⁷_____ slim.

Teacher: Thank you. Very good. Now, your homework today is to ⁸_____ some sentences about one person from your family and to ⁹_____ Exercise 6 on page 34.

Sam: When is it ¹⁰_____ ?

Teacher: For the next lesson, on Thursday.

8 Read the information and complete the sentences.

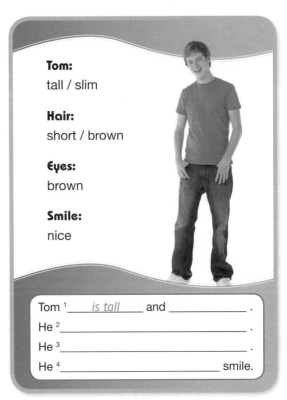

Tom:
tall / slim

Hair:
short / brown

Eyes:
brown

Smile:
nice

Tom ¹_____*is tall*_____ and _____ .
He ²_____ .
He ³_____ .
He ⁴_____ smile.

Anna and her sister:
short

Hair:
blond

Eyes:
blue

Appearance:
attractive

Natalie and her sister ⁵_____ .
They ⁶_____
and ⁷_____ .
⁸_____ attractive.

F Get Ready

1 Complete the lesson timetable.

Time	Lesson
Monday	
9.00	¹E n g l i s h
9.45	²i _ _ o r _ _ _ _ _ _ _ and c _ _ p _ _ _ _ _ t _ _ _ n _ _ _ _ _ 😊
10.30	³s c _ _ _ _ c _
11.15	⁴m _ _ _ _ s 🙁
12.00	⁵g _ _ g _ _ p _ _
12.45	LUNCH
1.30	⁶h _ _ t _ _ _
2.15	⁷p _ y _ _ _ _ _ e _ _ c _ _ _ _ _
3.00	HOME!!!

2 Complete the times with the correct words.

1	10.20	_twenty_ _past_	ten
2	4.15	_____ _____	four
3	10.45	_____ _____	eleven
4	7.30	_____ _____	seven
5	1.05	_____ _____	one
6	8.50	_____ _____	nine
7	6.00	six _____	
8	11.30	_____ _____ _____	

3 Choose the correct words to complete the dialogues.

Teacher: Work in pairs.
Brett: I haven't got a partner.
Chris and Dominika: You can work with ¹we/**us**/ours. ²We/Us/Our can be a group of three.
Emily: Where is Paul from?
Sue: I don't know. Ask ³he/him/his.
Teacher: Ask Anna a question.
Nicola: What?
Anna: Ask ⁴I/me/my a question.
Teacher: That's right. Ask ⁵she/her/hers a question and then tell ⁶we/us/ours the answer.
Dan: Where's ⁷I/me/my book?
Eric: Is this ⁸him/them/it?
Olivia: This is a photo of my sister.
Dana: ⁹She/He/It has got lovely red hair.
Olivia: Oh, no. That's not ¹⁰she/her/hers. That's ¹¹she/her/hers friend, Sandra.

4 Match the beginnings (1–8) with the correct endings (a–g). Two beginnings match with the same ending.

1 Can I go   _d_
2 Can I use   ___
3 Can I speak   ___
4 Can I open   ___
5 Can you spell   ___
6 Can you repeat   ___
7 Can you play   ___
8 What's *noir*   ___

a in my language, please?
b the CD again, please?
c in English?
d to the toilet, please?
e that, please?
f a dictionary?
g the window, please?

TOPIC TALK – VOCABULARY

1 Look at the pictures and complete the interests.

1 d <u>a n c i n g</u>

2 p _ _ _ _ g _ _ _ h _

3 r _ _ d _ _ _ _

4 t _ _ n _ _ _

5 c _ _ p _ _ _ _ g _ _ e _

6 f _ _ h _ _ _ _

7 f _ _ _ _ s

8 m _ _ i _

2 Complete the free time activities with the correct verb.

1 My name's Belinda. I b<u>uy</u> things online.
2 I'm Chris. I c_____ with my friends online.
3 Hi, I'm Dan. I d_____ lots of sport.
4 My name's Gary. I g_____ to the cinema on Saturdays.
5 I'm Lisa and I l_____ to music.
6 My name's Pete and I p_____ basketball.
7 Hello, I'm Rachel and, in the evening, I r_____ at home.
8 My name's William. I w_____ a lot of television.

3 Complete the text with the correct words.

My week
1_____*In*_____ the morning, I listen 2_____ music and eat breakfast. Then I go to school. In 3_____ afternoon, after school, I 4_____ shopping with my friends, then I go home and do my homework. In the evening, I 5_____ the internet. I play computer 6_____ or chat 7_____ my friends online.
8_____ Saturday, I 9_____ a lot of sport. I 10_____ football or go swimming. In the evening, I go 11_____ the cinema or parties. On Sunday, I relax 12_____ home and watch films.

4 Read the information and complete the sentences.

Monday - Friday:
7 a.m.	swimming
4 p.m.	running
9 p.m.	computer games

Saturday:
go out with my friends

Sunday:
homework, read

1 ____*In the*____ morning, I _go swimming_ .
2 _____ afternoon, I _____ .
3 _____ evening, I _____ .
4 _____ Saturday, _____ .
5 _____ Sunday, _____ .

13

GRAMMAR
Present Simple

1 * Complete the sentences with the correct form of the verbs below.

> chat   do   go   listen   live   love   ~~play~~   use

1 I _____play_____ tennis in the afternoon.
2 We _____ in a big house.
3 My brother _____ to parties every Saturday.
4 I _____ my homework in the evening.
5 My parents _____ the internet for their work.
6 My friends _____ online every day.
7 I _____ parties.
8 My dad _____ to music in the car.

2 ** Complete the text about Lisa's free time.

22 SEPTEMBER

My Day

In the morning, I go running. In the afternoon, I play tennis or basketball and then I do my homework. In the evening, I read and relax. On Saturday, I meet my friends. I go with them to parties or to the cinema. On Sunday, I use the internet. I chat online with my friends and I listen to music.

Lisa [1]_____goes_____ running in the morning. In the afternoon, she [2]_____ tennis or basketball and then she [3]_____ her homework. In the evening, she [4]_____ and [5]_____ . On Saturday, she [6]_____ her friends. She [7]_____ with them to parties or to the cinema. On Sunday, she [8]_____ the internet. She [9]_____ online with her friends and [10]_____ to music.

3 ** Complete the table with a positive or negative sentence.

Positive	Negative
1 We live in London.	_We don't live in London._
2 My friend likes maths.	_____
3 _____	My dad doesn't go swimming in the morning.
4 They know my cousin.	_____
5 _____	You don't work hard.
6 Paul goes to a private school.	_____
7 _____	My mum doesn't like pizza.

4 *** Correct the information in the sentences.

1 I play tennis. ✗ (football)
   I don't play tennis, I play football.
2 My sister likes computer games. ✗ (films)
   _____
3 My parents work in London. ✗ (Glasgow)
   _____
4 We learn Spanish at school. ✗ (French)
   _____
5 Your day starts at 6 o'clock. ✗ (7 o'clock)
   _____
6 Our teacher goes to the cinema on Sunday. ✗ (Saturday)
   _____
7 I do my homework at school. ✗ (home)
   _____
8 I chat online with my brother. ✗ (my friends)
   _____

Sentence Builder Adverbs of frequency

5 * **Rewrite the sentences with the adverb of frequency in the correct place.**

1 I go to the cinema in the morning. (never)
   I never go to the cinema in the morning.

2 My dad is tired. (often)
   _____

3 My sister buys things on the internet. (sometimes)
   _____

4 Our teachers are friendly. (usually)
   _____

5 My mum goes out. (often)
   _____

6 Discos are fun. (never)
   _____

7 My friends use the internet. (always)
   _____

8 My parents are busy. (often)
   _____

6 ** **Look at the information and complete sentences (1–5). Use** *always, never, often, sometimes* **and** *usually.*

	Monday	Tuesday	Wednesday	Thursday	Friday	Saturday	Sunday
1 Me – tired	✓	✗	✓	✗	✓	✗	✗
2 My brother – chat online	✓	✓	✓	✓	✓	✓	✓
3 My dad – eat breakfast	✓	✓	✗	✓	✓	✓	✓
4 My mum – go to discos	✗	✗	✗	✗	✗	✗	✗
5 My sister – watch TV	✓	✓	✓	✓	✗	✗	✓

1 Me – tired *I am sometimes tired.*
2 My brother _____
3 My dad _____
4 My mum _____
5 My sister _____

Grammar Alive Talking about habits

7 *** **Use the information to write sentences about habits.**

Use the internet:
   1 Cathy – never
   2 Me – often
   3 Sophie and Emma – sometimes

Play tennis:
   4 You – never
   5 Leo – sometimes
   6 Callum – often

Go shopping at the weekend:
   7 My parents – usually
   8 My sister – always
   9 Me – never

Watch horror films:
   10 My friends – sometimes
   11 My mum – never
   12 My dad – often

1 *Cathy never uses the internet.*
2 I _____
3 Sophie and Emma _____
4 You _____
5 Leo _____
6 Callum _____
7 My parents _____
8 My sister _____
9 I _____
10 My friends _____
11 My mum _____
12 My dad _____

Reading

1 **Read the text and choose one of the titles (1-3).**

1 The Yuma and other Native Americans.

2 My life with the Yuma.

3 Traditional Native American music.

home	about	search	sign up	travel

I am in Arizona in an area of the USA that is very near to Mexico. This is where the Yuma Native Americans live. There are about five hundred thousand Native American Indians in the USA. They are in different groups like the Yuma, Iroquois and Sioux and they speak about one hundred different languages. They don't live a really traditional lifestyle now. Some live in cities like Los Angeles and San Francisco. Others live in special Native American areas but they have modern homes.

San Francisco

Los Angeles

Arizona

Mexico

Some Yuma people live in traditional areas and keep their traditions and culture. Schools, colleges and museums teach the people about their history and lifestyle. Only about 400 of the Yuma people speak the Yuma language as their first language but the young people learn the language at school and they love listening to stories and songs in the language. Some of the men hunt small animals like rabbits but they usually buy their food from supermarkets like other Americans.

I am here because today there is a pow wow. This is a meeting of different Native American people. They sing traditional songs, have traditional dances, tell traditional stories and they cook traditional food. It's a great party and the people are very friendly to me and the other non-Native Americans here.

2 **Read the text again. Are the sentences true (T) or false (F)?**

1 The Yuma live in Arizona.   _T_

2 All Native Americans speak the same language.   ___

3 Native Americans who live in traditional areas live in traditional homes.   ___

4 Young Yuma people don't understand the Yuma language. ___

5 Native Americans only eat food that they hunt.   ___

6 People who aren't Native Americans can go to a *pow wow*.   ___

Sentence Builder *like* for examples

3 **Match the beginnings (1-5) with the correct endings (a-e).**

1 You can learn about groups of Native Americans   _b_

2 Native Americans can learn about their traditions in places   ___

3 Yuma men hunt animals   ___

4 At a *pow wow*, you can see traditional activities   ___

5 Many Native Americans now live in cities   ___

a like dancing and singing.

b like the Sioux, Iroquois and Yuma.

c like Los Angeles and San Francisco.

d like schools, colleges and museums.

e like rabbits.

4 Complete the sentences with *like* and the words below.

> basketball   vegetables   ~~French~~   Mexico
> Peru   ~~Spanish~~   tennis   meat

1 They speak many languages
  like French and Spanish.
2 On Saturday, we always play sports
  _____
3 They eat traditional foods
  _____
4 There are Native Indians in other countries
  _____

Listening

5 🔊 **2** Listen and complete the sentences with the correct word or number.

1 Arizona is in the USA near ___Canada___ .
2 There are _____ thousand Native Americans in the USA.
3 They speak about _____ languages.
4 Others live in special Native American areas in _____ .
5 They have schools, colleges and _____ .
6 Yuma students learn about their history and _____ .
7 There are about _____ people who still speak the Yuma language as their first language.
8 Some people hunt animals like _____ .
9 The speaker is there for a _____ .
10 You can see traditional singing and _____ .

6 Read the reading text on page 14 and the information in Exercise 5. Find five more things that the speaker said which are incorrect.

1 _Arizona is in the USA near ~~Canada~~. ✗ Mexico_
2 _____
3 _____
4 _____
5 _____
6 _____

Word Builder Plurals

7 Complete the sentences with the plural forms of the words in brackets.

1 Some Native Americans live in ____cities____ (city) like Los Angeles or San Francisco.
2 Native Americans speak many different _____ (language).
3 They don't live in traditional _____ (home).
4 Not many _____ (person) in my class speak Italian.
5 I like listening to _____ (story) about Native Americans.
6 Some of the _____ (man) in my town go hunting on Sundays.
7 _____ (Girl) and _____ (woman) like dancing and singing at _____ (party).
8 There are three _____ (bus) every hour from my house to the town centre.
9 My mum teaches young _____ (child) at a school in our village.

8 Complete the text with the correct plural of the words below.

> child   family   film   ~~friend~~   man
> party   phone   sport

Jake and I are very good [1]___friends___ . We like the same things. We both do [2]_____ like tennis and swimming and we both like watching [3]_____ and going to [4]_____ . Our [5]_____ are also friends. My mum and Jake's mum sometimes go to the cinema together and all the [6]_____ - our dads and their brothers, love talking about their computers and mobile [7]_____ . When we all meet, there are always a lot of young [8]_____ there because Jake has got three young brothers and a sister and I've got two sisters.

GRAMMAR
Present Simple: questions

1 * **Match the questions (1-6) with the answers (a-f).**

1 Do you often go online? _____b_
2 Does your brother play football? _____
3 Do your parents often go out? _____
4 Do you and your friends go to parties? _____
5 Does your sister like tennis? _____
6 Do I speak good English? _____

a No, she doesn't.
b Yes, I do.
c Yes, you do.
d No, they don't.
e No, he doesn't.
f Yes, we do.

2 ** **Use the cues to make questions and answers.**

1 How often / you go to the cinema?
never / go to the cinema
How often do you go to the cinema?
I never go to the cinema.

2 Where / your father work?
He / work / in London
_____
_____

3 When / you and your friends / meet?
meet / on Saturday afternoon
_____
_____

4 What / you do on the internet?
play games and chat with friends
_____
_____

5 How / your mum relax?
She / read
_____
_____

6 How often / your sister go online?
She always / go / online in the evening
_____
_____

7 What / your dad / do in the evenings?
He / watch / TV
_____
_____

8 What time / you / go to school?
I / go to school at eight o'clock
_____
_____

3 *** **Use the cues to complete the questions and short answers.**

1 (you / like) _Do you like_ parties?
(✓) _Yes, I do._

2 (your brother / buy things) _____ online?
(✗) _____

3 (your parents / watch) _____ television?
(✓) _____

4 (your mum / play) _____ a musical instrument?
(✓) _____

5 (your friends / go out) _____ on Sundays?
(✗) _____

6 (you and your brother / play) _____ computer games?
(✓) _____

7 (you / go) _____ to school by bus?
(✗) _____

Grammar Alive Asking about habits

4 ** **Complete the questions.**

1 A: What time ___ _do you eat breakfast?_ ___
   B: I eat breakfast at half past seven.
2 A: How often _____ ?
   B: I often play football.
3 A: How _____ ?
   B: I contact my friends by mobile phone.
4 A: When _____ ?
   B: I do my homework in the evening.
5 A: What sports _____ ?
   B: I play football, tennis and basketball.
6 A: What _____ ?
   B: I don't buy things online.

Speaking Workshop 1

1 **Choose the correct words to complete the dialogues.**

  1 **A:** How ¹*old are / are / do* you?

    B: I'm ²*right / nice / fine* thanks.

  2 **A:** Hello, my name's Elaine.

    B: Hi ³*there / here / then*. Nice to ⁴*find / meet / look* you.

  3 **A:** ⁵*Meet / See / Hear* you later.

    B: ⁶*Bye / Hi / Hello*. ⁷*Make / Do / Have* a good time.

    A: ⁸*Too / And / For* you.

2 **Complete the conversation below with Dan's part of the conversation (a-f).**

  a Hi Steve. How are you?

  b Paula, Laura. This is Steve. Steve, this is Laura and Paula.

  c Hi there. My name's Dan.

  d And who's this?

  e That's Paula and Laura. Do you want to meet them?

  f Good to meet you, Laura. Oh, there's my friend, Steve. We play the guitar together. See you later.

  1 **Dan:**   *Hi there. My name's Dan.*

    Paula: Hello. Pleased to meet you. I'm Paula.

  2 **Dan:** _____

    Paula: Oh, this is my friend, Laura.

  3 **Dan:** _____

    Paula: Okay. Bye, Dan.

    ...

  4 **Dan:** _____

    Steve: I'm fine, thanks. Who are those girls?

  5 **Dan:** _____

    Steve: Yes, of course.

    ...

  6 **Dan:** _____

    Steve: Hi, good to meet you.

3   3 and 4   **Listen to someone talking (1-4) and choose the correct response (a-d). Then listen to check your answers.**

  a I'm fine, thanks.

  b Hi there. Pleased to meet you.

  c Bye.

  d And you.

  1 ___

  2 ___

  3 ___

  4 ___

4   5   **Complete the dialogue. Listen and check your answers.**

  Dave: Good morning, Gary, ¹____*How*____ are you?

  Gary: I'm ²_____ , thanks. ³_____ is my friend, Bob. It's his first time today.

  Dave: Great. Hello Bob. My name's Dave.

  Bob: Hi ⁴_____ . Nice to ⁵_____ you.

  Dave: Bob – can you write your name and address here, please?

  Bob: Okay.

  Dave: How ⁶_____ are you?

  Bob: I'm sixteen.

  Dave: Can you swim?

  Bob: Yes, I can.

  Dave: Good. This is Michelle. Our new teacher here.

  Michelle: ⁷_____ there.

  Gary: Nice ⁸_____ meet you, Michelle!

  Bob: Hi, ⁹_____ to meet you.

Writing Workshop 1

1 Read the letter. Put the paragraphs (A-D) in the correct order.

Hi Adrian,

A ___ I go to Morava High School. It's a small school but there are lots of activities to do after lessons finish like sports ¹___*and*___ film making. We start early, at eight o'clock, but we usually finish at one o'clock in the afternoon. I do my homework and then I read ²_____ watch TV. Sometimes I chat to my old friends from Prague.

B _1_ Thanks for your email. How are you and your family? We are in our new house in Znojmo. It's great.

C ___ How is your new school? Please write and tell me about your teachers and school friends.

D ___ Znojmo is a very old town. It's very beautiful ³_____ interesting. We've got a house near the centre. On Saturdays, I go to the town ⁴_____ meet my friends at a café. On Sundays we usually go for a walk in Znojmo ⁵_____ visit our cousins in Brno.

Write soon,
Jan

2 Complete the letter with *and/or*.

3 Match the beginnings (1-8) with the endings (a-h).

1 We go to the cinema   _d_
2 I want to be a teacher   ___
3 At 10 p.m. I have a shower ___
4 Our teacher is kind   ___
5 I clean my room on Saturdays ___
6 The town is old   ___
7 I can play the piano   ___
8 I eat breakfast at home   ___

a or Sundays.
b and go to bed.
c and friendly.
d or a cafe.
e and the guitar.
f or when I get to school.
g and beautiful.
h or a doctor when I leave school.

4 Complete the sentences with the words in capitals.

1 COFFEE / EAT BREAKFAST
   a In the morning, I drink tea and *eat breakfast.*
   b In the morning, I drink tea or ___*coffee.*___
2 CAR / WALK HOME
   a I go to school by bus or _____
   b I go to school by bus and _____
3 DO MY HOMEWORK / PLAY SPORTS AT SCHOOL
   a In the afternoon, I go home or _____
   b In the afternoon, I go home and _____
4 THE SWIMMING POOL / DRINK COLA WITH THEM
   a On Saturday, I meet me friends at a café and
      _____
   b On Saturday, I meet my friends at a café or
      _____
5 MONDAY AND FRIDAY / MONDAY OR FRIDAY
   a We get homework once a week on
      _____
   b We get homework twice a week on
      _____

5 Complete the sentences with *and/or* and the words and phrases below.

~~eat~~   go shopping   have eight lessons every day
      a television   a football match   they visit us

1 I go to school by bus ___*or car.*___ .
2 We start school at nine o'clock _____ .
3 I've got a computer _____ in my room.
4 At 8.45 p.m. on Wednesdays, I watch a film _____ on TV.
5 On Saturdays, I meet my friends _____ with them.
6 On Sundays, we visit our cousins _____ .

6 Write a reply to Jan in Exercise 1. Write about these things:

* Thank him for his email
* Tell him about your new school
* Tell him about your free time
* End the letter and ask him to tell you about Czech music and films.

Sound Choice 1

Sound Check

Say the words and expressions below.

a plays, works, relaxes (Exercise 1)
b we're, they've, don't (Exercise 2)
c swim, sport, story (Exercise 3)
d bad, sad, am, men, when, bed (Exercise 4)
e swimming, running, village (Exercise 5)
f How are you? See you later! (Exercise 6)
g earrings, Wednesday, fifteen (Exercise 7)

6 Listen and check your answers. Which sounds and expressions did you have problems with? Choose three exercises to do below.

Grammar

1 **7** Grammar – 3rd person -s **Write the words below in the correct column depending on the sound of the final -s. Then listen and check.**

play work relax watch look go ~~wake~~
buy use

/s/	/z/	/ɪz/
chats	does	matches
wakes	_____	_____
_____	_____	_____
_____	_____	_____

2 **8** Grammar – Contractions **Listen and write the words.**

1 _we're_   5 _____
2 _____   6 _____
3 _____   7 _____
4 _____

3 **9** Consonants **Write the first two letters of the words you hear.**

1 _sw_   3 _____   5 _____
2 _____   4 _____   6 _____

4 **10** Vowels **Tick (✓) the words you hear.**

1 bad ✓   bed ☐
2 man ☐   men ☐
3 woman ☐   women ☐
4 had ☐   head ☐
5 pan ☐   pen ☐

5 **11** Double consonants **Listen and write the consonant which is doubled.**

1 _m_   4 __   7 __
2 __   5 __   8 __
3 __   6 __

6 **12** Expressions **Listen and repeat the expressions.**

1 How are you?
2 See you later.
3 My name's Tom.
4 This is my friend, Chris.
5 Have a good time.
6 And you.

7 **13** Difficult words **Listen to the words below. Write them in the correct column depending on their stress pattern.**

~~racket~~ earrings Wednesday online quarter
fashion tennis fifteen relax

Oo	oO
racket	_____
_____	_____
_____	_____
_____	
_____	

Check Your Progress 1

1 My interests **Complete the sentences with the words below. There are four extra words.**

> buy chat do fashion games have listen
> make out play relax sports use watch

1 I often _____ things online.
2 My brother buys a lot of computer _____ .
3 In the evening, my friends and I _____ online.
4 I do a lot of _____ like basketball, tennis and football.
5 I like going _____ with my friends on Saturdays.
6 Do you often _____ to music?
7 I want to _____ basketball today.
8 When I'm tired, I _____ at home.
9 Do you _____ a lot of films?
10 I _____ the internet every day.

/10

2 Present Simple **Complete the sentences with the correct form of the verbs in brackets.**

1 My dad _____ (love) football.
2 How often _____ (you / listen) to music?
3 _____ (your / mum) go running?
4 I _____ (not play) computer games.
5 My friends often _____ (go) to the cinema.
6 Lana _____ (watch) TV every day.
7 Sam _____ (not speak) French.
8 What films _____ (you watch)?
9 We _____ (not know) the answer.
10 My friend's dad _____ (hunt) wild animals.

/10

3 Adverbs of frequency **Put the sentences in the correct order.**

1 school / nine o'clock / We / at / start / usually

_____

2 interesting / lessons / are / Our / always

_____

3 sometimes / home / My dad / from work / late / comes

_____

4 on / never / Monday morning / My friends / happy / are

_____

5 usually / I / coffee / the morning / in / drink

_____

/5

4 Plurals **Complete the sentences with the correct plural of the words below.**

> bus child house life party

1 There were twelve _____ at the party. Six boys and six girls.
2 My dad's brother is very rich. He's got three _____ , one in London, one in France and one in Spain.
3 There are two _____ from my house to the swimming pool. Number 6 and number 9.
4 I like reading about Native Americans. Their _____ and traditions are very interesting.
5 There are two _____ this weekend – one on Sunday and one on Saturday.

/5

5 Meeting people **Complete the dialogues with the correct words.**

A: Hello, Steve. ¹_____ are you?
B: I'm fine, thanks.

A: David. This is my friend Chris. Chris, this is David.
B: Hi, Chris. Pleased to ²_____ you.

A: Hello. My name's Rosy.
B: Hi ³_____ . Good to meet you.

A: See you later.
B: Bye. ⁴_____ a good time.
A: ⁵_____ you.

/5

TOTAL SCORE **/35**

Module Diary 1

1 **Look at the objectives on page 11 in the Students' Book. Choose three and evaluate your learning.**

1 Now I can _____ well / quite well / with problems.
2 Now I can _____ well / quite well / with problems.
3 Now I can _____ well / quite well / with problems.

2 **Look at your results. What language areas in this module do you need to study more?**

TOPIC TALK – VOCABULARY

1 Look at the clues and find the words.

¹S	o	f	a	
	²c	u		
³w		r		
⁴w		n		
⁵c		i		
		⁶t		
	⁷c	u		
⁸f		r		
	⁹d	e		

1 Two or three people can sit on this.
2 You can put things in this.
3 You put your clothes here.
4 You can look out of this.
5 You sit on this.
6 You put things on this.
7 You open these in the morning and close them in the evening.
8 You walk on this.
9 Have you got a computer on this in your bedroom?

2 Write the rooms.

1 We watch TV and relax in the l*iving* r*oom* .
2 We cook in the k_____ .
3 I wash in the b_____ .
4 We eat in the d_____ r_____ .
5 I sleep in my b_____ .
6 When you come into the house, you are in the h_____ .

3 Choose the correct words to complete the sentences.

1 The pizza is in the _b_ .
   a wardrobe   **b** oven   **c** dishwasher
2 The cola is in the ___ .
   a fridge   **b** cooker   **c** carpet
3 Put your clothes into the ___ .
   a dishwasher   **b** fridge
   c washing machine
4 The picture is on the ___ .
   a floor   **b** wall   **c** plant
5 Look at your hair in the ___ .
   a wall   **b** fridge   **c** mirror
6 We can have dinner in five minutes now that we've got a ___ .
   a microwave   **b** oven   **c** cooker
7 Give the ___ some water.
   a lamp   **b** plant   **c** curtains
8 Close the ___ when you go out.
   a door   **b** computer   **c** bookshelf

4 Complete the text with the words below.

~~bedrooms~~ bookshelves carpet comfortable
favourite relax walls windows

I like my house. It has got three ¹ _bedrooms_ .
Mine is small but it's very ² _____ . It's my
³ _____ room in the house. It's a great place
to ⁴ _____ . The ⁵ _____ in my room
are white and there are two big ⁶ _____ so it
is very light. I've got a desk, a computer, a wardrobe
and a red ⁷ _____ on the floor. There are also
some ⁸ _____ . I keep my CDs on them.

4 GRAMMAR
there is/are, some/any

1 * Complete the sentences with *there is* or *there are*.

1 ___There is___ a big poster on the wall.
2 _____ a desk in my bedroom.
3 _____ some books on the desk.
4 _____ some nice curtains in the living room.
5 _____ two chairs in the kitchen.
6 _____ three CDs in my bag.
7 _____ two people in the room.
8 _____ a kitchen and a living room.

2 * Choose the correct word to complete the sentences.

1 There are (some)/any plants.
2 There aren't *some/any* carpets.
3 Are there *some/any* pictures in that book?
4 Is there *a/any* cooker?
5 There is *some/a* microwave.
6 There isn't *a/any* dishwasher.
7 Are there *some/any* mirrors?
8 Is there *any/a* fridge?

3 ** Complete the sentences. Make them positive (+) or negative (-).

1 ___There are some___ CDs on the desk. (+)
2 _____ table in the kitchen. (+)
3 _____ computers in our classroom. (-)
4 _____ photos on my wall. (-)
5 _____ television in my room. (-)
6 _____ lamp on my desk. (-)
7 _____ spider in the bathroom. (+)
8 _____ cupboards in the kitchen. (+)

4 ** Make full sentences from the cues.

1 ✓ / two chairs / in my bedroom
   There are two chairs in my bedroom.
2 ✓ / pen / on my desk
   _____
3 ✗ / clothes / on my floor
   _____
4 ✗ / mirror / in the living room
5 ✓ / MP3 player / in my bag
   _____
6 ✗ / CDs / on the desk
   _____
7 ✓ / people / in the kitchen
   _____
8 ✗ / clock / on my wall
   _____

5 ** Complete the text with the words below.

a any are aren't is
isn't some there

This is my bedroom. There [1] ___is___ a window. It's very big. Near the window, there is [2]_____ desk. It isn't very tidy! There [3]_____ some books on the desk and [4]_____ is a computer. There aren't [5]_____ CDs but there is an MP3 player. There are [6]_____ clothes on the floor and on the bed because there [7]_____ a wardrobe in my bedroom. The wardrobe is in my parents' bedroom. There [8]_____ any posters on the walls. I haven't got any.

6 ** Choose the correct words to complete the sentences.

1 There _b_ any songs on my MP3 player.
   a isn't   b aren't   c are

2 There ___ some bookshelves in the living room.
   a are   b isn't   c is

3 There ___ a computer on my desk. I haven't got one.
   a is   b are   c isn't

4 Is there ___ carpet in your living room?
   a any   b some   c a

5 Are there ___ books in your bag?
   a any   b a   c some

6 There aren't ___ good films on TV.
   a some   b any   c a

7 There isn't ___ wardrobe in my bedroom.
   a a   b some   c any

8 There ___ a fridge in the kitchen. It's big and white.
   a is   b are   c isn't

9 There are ___ Italian students in our school.
   a an   b some   c any

10 ___ any good films at the cinema?
   a Are there   b There are   c Is there

7 *** Use the cues to write sentences and questions.

1 windows - in the kitchen?
Are there any windows in the kitchen?

2 no dictionaries - on the bookshelf
_____

3 mobile phone - in your bag?
_____

4 guitar - on your bed
_____

5 no teacher - in the classroom
_____

6 new fridge - in the kitchen?
_____

7 songs - on your computer
_____

8 good shoes - in this shop
_____

Grammar Alive Describing rooms

8 *** Use the information to make questions and answers.

1 A: carpet / in your room?
   B: ✓ - brown
   Is there a carpet in your room?
   Yes, there is a brown carpet.

2 A: posters / on your walls?
   B: ✓ - three
   _____
   _____

3 A: chairs / in your room?
   B: ✓ - one
   _____
   _____

4 A: plant / in your room?
   B: ✗
   _____
   _____

5 A: books / on your desk
   B: ✗ - but / some on the shelves
   _____
   _____

6 A: guitar / on your bed
   B: ✓ - red
   _____
   _____

7 A: TV / in your room
   B: ✗ - but / a computer
   _____
   _____

8 A: table / in your kitchen
   B: ✓ - and six chairs
   _____
   _____

9 A: mirror / in your bedroom
   B: ✗ - but / one in the bathroom
   _____
   _____

SKILLS

Reading

1 Match the words (1-8) with the pictures (a-h).

1 Temperature _c_
2 cup of tea ___
3 shower ___
4 mirror ___
5 fridge ___
6 street ___
7 car wash ___
8 sleep ___

2 Read the text and match the machines (1-6) with the things they do (a-i). Three machines match with two things.

1 Smart bed _d_
2 Smart mirror ___
3 Smart shower ___
4 Smart fridge ___
5 Smart TV ___
6 Smart robot ___

a It orders our food.
b It speaks to my sister.
c It looks after the dog.
d It controls the temperature.
e It speaks to me.
f It stops after five minutes.
g It doesn't listen to other people.
h It makes me a cup of tea.
i It speaks to my family.

Word Builder Multi-part verbs (1)

3 Complete the sentences with the correct words.

1 My bed is always warm when I ____go____ to bed.
2 My little brother often _____ up in the night and goes to my parents' bedroom.
3 I look _____ my little brother when my parents go _____ in the evening.
4 My dad works hard. He never gets _____ home from work before 9 p.m.
5 I read in bed for thirty minutes and then I go _____ sleep.
6 When I get _____ , I open the curtains.

My dream smart home ...

The bedroom: When I go to bed, the smart bed automatically gets warm. When I am asleep it controls the temperature. In the morning, when I wake up, my robot makes me a cup of tea. I drink the tea in bed and then get up.

The bathroom has got a smart shower. When my sister is in the shower, it stops after five minutes and says to her, 'Your brother wants to use the bathroom now.' The smart mirror says nice things to me like, 'Your hair is great today!'

The kitchen has got a smart fridge. It orders food from the internet. My smart fridge orders food for all my family and it knows our favourite food. It talks to my family. It says, 'Don't eat that, it's John's!'

The living room: The smart TV knows what I like and it finds things that I want to watch. It doesn't listen to other people.

My dog: My smart robot looks after the dog. It gives him food and it takes him out for exercise.

4 Look at the pictures and complete the sentences.

1

I _____get up_____ at 6.40 a.m.

2

My mum _____ at ten o'clock.

3

I _____ at 6.30 a.m.

4

I _____ home from school at four o'clock.

5

My parents _____ at 10.30 p.m.

Sentence Builder Prepositions of place: *in/on/at*

5 Put the words below in the correct columns.

~~your bag~~   school   the shelves   my desk   Spain
work   the fridge   the wall   a party   my bedroom
home   the floor

in	at	on
your bag	_____	_____
_____	_____	_____
_____	_____	_____
_____	_____	_____

6 Complete the text with the correct words.

We have English lessons [1]_____in_____ room 18. There are twenty desks for students and one desk for the teacher. [2]_____ the walls, there are lots of posters of England. There's a cupboard at the front of the room and [3]_____ the cupboard, there's a TV and DVD player. Sometimes we watch films. There are some bookshelves in the classroom. [4]_____ the shelves, there are a lot of English books. Our books are [5]_____ the teacher's desk. He wants to look at our homework. His bag is [6]_____ the floor and there is some food [7]_____ the bag. It's now 4 p.m. We are [8]_____ home but our teacher is [9]_____ school. He often stays late. I think he likes room 18.

7 Match the beginnings with the correct endings.

1

1 My guitar is in	_b_	**a** my bed.
2 My guitar is at	___	**b** my bedroom.
3 My guitar is on	___	**c** school.

2

1 Dad is at	___	**a** his desk at work.
2 Dad's phone is on	___	**b** the hall.
3 Dad's coat is in	___	**c** work.

3

1 There are some posters on	___	**a** my bedroom wall.
2 There are some posters in	___	**b** home.
3 There are some posters at	___	**c** our classroom.

8 Use the cues to make sentences.

1 my classroom / pictures / the walls ✓
In my classroom, there are some pictures on the wall.

2 books / the desk / my bedroom ✗
_____

3 At the moment / my dad / work ✗
_____

4 food / fridge / our kitchen ✓
_____

5 At the moment / I / home ✓
_____

6 a mobile phone / my bag ✗
_____

7 At the moment / mum / shops ✓
_____

8 clothes / the floor / my bedroom ✗
_____

GRAMMAR
Countable/Uncountable nouns and *a lot of/no*

1 * Put the words below in the correct column.

~~books~~ children food furniture men people
rooms space time water

countable	uncountable
books	_____
_____	_____
_____	_____
_____	_____
_____	_____

2 ** Choose the correct words to complete the sentences.

1 How *much/many* time have you got?
2 *Is/Are* there a lot of furniture in your bedroom?
3 There *are/aren't* no pictures on the wall.
4 There is *any/no* space for a desk.
5 How *much/many* chairs are there in the classroom?
6 How much water *is/are* there?
7 *Is/Are* there many books on the shelf?
8 Is there *much/many* food to eat?

3 *** Complete the letter with the words below. There are four extra words.

a   are   aren't   how   is   ~~isn't~~   lot   many
much (x 2)   no   of   some

Dear Craig,

Hi. How are you? I like my room here at university. There ¹_____isn't_____ much space and there isn't ²_____ furniture but I've got a bed and a desk. I'm not here very often. We have a ³_____ of lessons every day.

There is one chair but there are ⁴_____ armchairs or sofas. My friends sit on the bed when they visit me. I've got ⁵_____ lot of friends here and there ⁶_____ a lot of things to do in the evening.

Thanks for the letter and the computer game. How ⁷_____ new games have you got? I don't play games very often here. I haven't got ⁸_____ time to relax. We get lots ⁹_____ homework in the evening.

Hope you're okay. See you soon.
Adrian

Grammar Alive Talking about quantity

4 *** Use the cues to make questions with *How much* and *How many*. Use *is/are there* or *have you got*. Use the cues to write answers.

1 people / your family (there / four)
   How many people are there in your family?
   There are four people in my family.

2 CDs / your room (have / seventeen)
   _____
   _____

3 water / your fridge (there / a lot)
   _____
   _____

4 money / your bag (have / £10)
   _____
   _____

5 books / your desk (there / two)
   _____
   _____

6 time / before you go to bed (have / an hour)
   _____
   _____

7 boys / your class (there / twelve)
   _____
   _____

Speaking Workshop 2

1 Match the feelings (1–8) with the correct pictures (a–h).

1	sad	_c_	
2	tired	___	
3	scared	___	
4	happy	___	
5	angry	___	
6	hungry	___

Talk Builder Suggestions

2 Choose the correct words to complete the sentences.

1 **A:** Why _a_ we go out?

    a don't   **b** aren't   **c** not

    B: Good ___ .

    a time   **b** reason   **c** idea

2 **A:** Let's ___ TV.

    a to watch   **b** watching   **c** watch

    B: All ___ .

    a right   **b** good   **c** okay

3 Do you want to go out? I'm not ___ .

    a right   **b** sure   **c** want to

3 Complete the dialogue with the correct words.

Luke: Sam's very excited about his holiday. ¹ _Let's_ ask him about it.

Toby: All ² _____ . Hey, Sam. Have you got your holiday photos here?

Sam: No, they're on my computer at home.

Toby: ³ _____ don't ⁴ _____ bring them to school?

Sam: I'm not ⁵ _____ . I don't really ⁶ _____ to. I'm worried about my computer. Why don't you come to my house one day?

Toby: Okay, good ⁷ _____ . Let's go after school.

Sam: Okay.

4 〔14〕 Use the cues to complete the dialogue. Then listen to check.

1 Emma: Here's a text from Mum. Home at six. Pizza for dinner. Do your homework, please.

    Zoe: I've got an exam on Monday. You've got your homework. ¹ _So let's start._ (So / let / start)

    Emma: No, ² _____ . (I / not want)
³ _____ . (tired)

    Zoe: Where's my schoolbag?

    Emma: ⁴ _____ . (bored) Hey, ⁵ _____ (let / go) on the computer.

2 Emma: Tom is so funny! There's a photo of him on the computer. Come and look!

    Zoe: ⁶ _____ . (not interested) ⁷ _____ (Why / you chat) to your friends online? Or listen to music? Or read a book?

    Emma: Hmm, ⁸ _____ . (no / sure)

3 Zoe: ⁹ _____ (Why / play) a computer game? That new one you've got.

    Emma: Yeah. ¹⁰ _____ . (idea)

    Zoe: Emma, it's nearly six o'clock. And I'm hungry! ¹¹ _____ (Why / lay) the table for dinner?

    Emma: ¹² _____ . (All / right) ¹³ _____ (let / have) some flowers … ta da!

Exam Choice 1

Reading

1 Read the text and choose the best title.

1 My new house ___
2 Buy a house ___
3 House problems ___

House in Tonbridge only fifty kilometres from London.

£150,000

The house has got two bedrooms, a kitchen, a living room and a bathroom. The kitchen is blue with white cupboards. There's a big fridge and a modern cooker. There isn't a dishwasher but there's lots of space for a table and six chairs. You can eat in here because there isn't a dining room. The living room has got two very big windows and it is very light and comfortable. There is a sofa and two armchairs and some shelves on one wall. One bedroom is big with a wardrobe. The second is small with no furniture.

It's a great place to live for people who like sports. You can go running or play tennis near the house. It's great for children too as it is only fifty metres from the school.

The house has got gas and electricity. The cooker uses gas and the hot water uses electricity. There aren't any carpets but there are a lot of things here for you. Come to see the house now.

< >

2 Match the things in the house (1-5) with the descriptions (a-f).

1 The hot water ___
2 The cooker ___
3 The living room ___
4 The fridge ___
5 The small bedroom ___

a It hasn't got any furniture.
b It's big.
c It uses gas.
d It uses electricity.
e It's modern.
f It's got two big windows.

3 Read the text again. Are the sentences true (T) or false (F)?

1 The house is in London. ___
2 There are five rooms in the house. ___
3 Six people can sit in the kitchen. ___
4 There isn't any furniture in the living room. ___
5 There are two big bedrooms. ___
6 The house is near to a school. ___

Listening

4 🔊 15 Listen to someone at the house in Tonbridge and find six things different to the reading text. Write (S), if the information is the same in the listening and reading. Write the new information if the listening is different.

1 The kitchen is blue. _____
2 The cupboards are white. _____
3 The fridge is big. _____
4 The cooker is modern. _____
5 There is space for six chairs. _____
6 The living room is light. _____
7 There are two armchairs. _____
8 There are some shelves. _____
9 There is a wardrobe in one bedroom. _____
10 The school is fifty metres from the house. _____
11 The cooker uses gas. _____

Speaking

5 Complete the dialogue with the phrases below.

And you   Have a good time   How are you
I'm not sure   Let's meet   Pleased to meet you
See you   This is   Why don't you

Jack: Hi Chris. ¹_____ ?
Chris: Hi Jack. I'm fine, thanks.
Jack: Good. Chris, ²_____ Hannah.
Chris: Hi there, Hannah. ³_____ .
Hannah: Hi.
Jack: Chris, there's a good film on at the cinema. ⁴_____ come with us?
Chris: ⁵_____ . I want to go to the new swimming pool with Mick and Terry. ⁶_____ on Sunday.
Jack: Okay. Good idea. ⁷_____ later.
Chris: Bye. ⁸_____ .
Jack: Thanks. ⁹_____ .

Use of English

6 Choose the correct words to complete the sentences.

1 I like ___ with my friends online.
   a chatting   **b** using   **c** listening
2 My mum ___ often go out in the evening.
   a isn't   **b** don't   **c** doesn't
3 I do a lot of sports ___ tennis, swimming and basketball.
   a like   **b** example   **c** play
4 Do you like going to parties? Yes, I ___ .
   a am   **b** do   **c** like
5 Cook the meat in the ___ for five minutes.
   a fridge   **b** wardrobe   **c** microwave
6 It's a beautiful day. Open the ___ .
   a carpets   **b** curtains   **c** walls

7 Complete the text with the correct words.

I wake [1]_____ at seven o'clock in the morning. I have a shower [2]_____ eat breakfast. I go to school at half past eight. There [3]_____ a bus to school but I usually meet my friends and walk. I [4]_____ back home at four o'clock and do my homework. [5]_____ the evening, I watch TV [6]_____ play computer games. I go [7]_____ bed at eleven o'clock.

I have a [8]_____ of free time at the weekend. Our teacher is very nice to us and she doesn't give us [9]_____ homework on Fridays! No homework at all! I always go [10]_____ with my friends but we haven't got [11]_____ money so we buy a small drink and sit in the café for two or three hours. There are [12]_____ nice cafés in our town.

Writing

8 Use the cues to make sentences.

1 There / kitchen / living room / three bedrooms. There / not / dining room

   _____

2 There / lot / posters / the walls / my bedroom

   _____

3 have got / a big desk / my room

   _____

4 There / not / shelves / my room. My books / the floor

   _____

5 It / great place / relax

   _____

9 You live in a new house. Write a letter to a friend. Tell your friend:

- How many rooms there are in the house
- What you have got in your room

Check Your Progress 2

1 My home **Complete the names of furniture and other things that you find in the house.**

Kitchen
1 _ o _ k _ _
2 f _ _ d _ e
Bathroom
3 _ h _ w _ _
4 m _ r _ _ _
Living room
5 _ _ f _
6 a _ _ c h _ _ r
Bedroom
7 w _ r _ r _ _ e

/7

2 *there is/are* and *some/any* **Complete the questions and answers.**

1 **A:** pens / on your desk?
   B: No / but / pencils.
   A: ¹_____ on your desk?
   B: No, ²_____ but ³_____ pencils.
2 **A:** a microwave / in the kitchen?
   B: Yes / and / a cooker
   A: ⁴_____ in the kitchen?
   B: Yes, ⁵_____ and ⁶_____ a cooker.
3 **A:** books / in the living room?
   B: Yes / but / no shelves
   A: ⁷_____
   B: Yes, ⁸_____ but ⁹_____ shelves.

/9

3 Multi-part verbs (1) **Complete the sentences with the correct words. You can see the first letter of each word.**

1 What time do you w_____ u_____ in the morning?
2 I hate mornings. I stay in bed for about half an hour before I g_____ u_____ and go to the bathroom.
3 I usually meet my friends on Saturday. I g_____ o_____ at about two o'clock in the afternoon and I g_____ b_____ home in the evening.
4 I go to bed at about eleven o'clock but I don't g_____ t_____ s_____ . I read.
5 Sometimes my grandmother comes to our house to l_____ a_____ my little brother.

/6

4 Prepositions of place **Choose the correct word to complete the sentences.**

1 My sister is *in/at/on* home *in/at/on* her room.
2 My clothes are *in/at/on* the floor, not *in/on/at* my wardrobe.
3 My mum is *in/at/on* work and my dad is *in/on/at* the shops.
4 My books are *in/at/on* my desk but my pen is *in/on/at* my bag.
5 Dinner isn't *in/at/on* the oven. It's *in/at/on* the table.

/5

5 countable/uncountable nouns, *a lot of/no, How much/How many* **Complete the dialogues with the correct words.**

A: How ¹_____ students ²_____ there in your class?
B: There ³_____ twenty-four students in my class.
A: How ⁴_____ free time do you usually have after school?
B: I have ⁵_____ free time ☹. We get a ⁶_____ of homework and I also help my parents at home. I never have time to watch TV or play computer games.
A: ⁷_____ there ⁸_____ food I can eat?
B: Sorry, there's no food in the house, I'm afraid.

/8

TOTAL SCORE **/35**

Module Diary 2

1 **Look at the objectives on page 21 in the Students' Book. Choose three and evaluate your learning.**

1 Now I can _____ well / quite well / with problems.
2 Now I can _____ well / quite well / with problems.
3 Now I can _____ well / quite well / with problems.

2 **Look at your results. What language areas in this module do you need to study more?**

TOPIC TALK - VOCABULARY

1 Recommend the best place to go (a-f) for each of the people (1-6).

1 I'm hungry. `c`

2 I'd like a drink. ☐

3 I need a new skirt. ☐

4 I want to learn about the history of our town. ☐

5 I'd like to see John in *Romeo and Juliet*. ☐

6 I want to see a film. ☐

a theatre
b shops
c restaurant
d cinema
e café
f museum

2 Complete the sentences with the words below.

café centre (x 2) club ~~market~~ park (x 2) pool

1 You can find interesting things to buy in the outdoor ___market___ .
2 John and Matt have gone to the swimming _____ .
3 There are a lot of great shops in the shopping _____ .
4 We can have a coffee at an outdoor _____ .
5 We had a great time at the new amusement _____ .
6 Let's go dancing at the new night _____ .
7 You can play tennis, basketball and other sports at the sports _____ .
8 Now I've got a skateboard, I want to go to the skate _____ .

3 Choose the correct words to complete the sentences.

1 There's nothing to do here. It's _b_ .
   a exciting   b boring   c interesting
2 I love the new cinema. The seats are so ___ .
   a comfortable b friendly   c expensive
3 50p for a ticket. That's really ___ .
   a busy   b cheap   c friendly
4 The museum was really ___ . I learned a lot.
   a interesting b cheap   c boring
5 I like this café because the people who work here are very ___ .
   a noisy   b comfortable c friendly
6 Don't go shopping on Saturday afternoon. The shops are really ___ .
   a relaxed   b busy   c exciting
7 I don't like nightclubs because they are very ___ . I can't hear my friends when they talk to me.
   a noisy   b expensive   c relaxed
8 It's a nice restaurant but it's very ___ . There are only three tables.
   a busy   b friendly   c small

4 Complete the sentences with the phrases below.

aren't any   because it is   busy and expensive   good cafes   I love   ~~in my town~~   my favourite place   our local

1 _In my town,_ there are a lot of _____ .
2 There _____ good shops.
3 _____ cinemas and nightclubs.
4 _____ is an outdoor market in my town.
5 I like it _____ very interesting and cheap.
6 I don't like _____ shopping centre because it is very _____ .

1 * Complete the sentences with the correct form of the adjectives in brackets.

1 Our theatre is _____bigger_____ (big) than our cinema.

2 Museums are _____ (interesting) than art galleries.

3 The market is _____ (cheap) than the shopping centre.

4 The amusement park is _____ (noisy) than the swimming pool.

5 The French restaurant in our town is _____ (expensive) than the Italian restaurant.

6 Sundays are _____ (boring) than Saturdays.

7 My mum is _____ (relaxed) than my dad.

8 My new school is _____ (modern) than my old school.

2 * Complete the dialogue with the words below.

are   better   busier   is   more (x 2)   quieter   than

Nick: Which restaurant do you want to go to?

Ellie: I don't know. The Chinese restaurant [1]_____is_____ cheaper than the Italian restaurant. We can go there.

Nick: But Italian food is nicer [2]_____ Chinese food.

Ellie: I know but I'm worried about money. The Italian restaurant is [3]_____ expensive and I haven't got much money.

Nick: We can have a pizza. That isn't expensive. Come on. I like Enzo's. The waiters [4]_____ much friendlier than the waiters in Kong Fu.

Ellie: Yes, but can we get a table? It's much [5]_____ than Kong Fu. I like Kong Fu because it's [6]_____ and [7]_____ relaxed.

Nick: That's because Enzo's is [8]_____ than Kong Fu. Let's have a pizza today and eat Chinese food next week.

Ellie: Okay. Good idea.

3a ** Match the adjectives (1–7) with their opposites (a–i).

1 big _____f_____   **a** bad

2 boring _____   **b** cheap

3 good _____   **c** light

4 expensive _____   **d** modern

5 old _____   **e** noisy

6 quiet _____   **f** small

7 dark _____   **g** busy

h exciting

i new

3b ** Complete the second sentence with the correct form of the opposite adjective.

1 The museum is bigger than the art gallery.
The art gallery _____is smaller than_____ the museum.

2 The sports centre is more expensive than the swimming pool
The swimming pool _____ the sports centre.

3 The market is older than the shopping centre.
The shopping centre _____ the market.

4 The skate park is busier than the amusement park.
The amusement park _____ the skate park.

5 The food here is worse than my cooking!
My cooking _____ the food here!

6 The dining room is darker than the living room.
The living room _____ the dining room.

7 I'm quieter than my brother.
My brother _____ I am.

8 My computer is newer than my mobile phone.
My mobile phone _____ my computer.

4 *** **Use the cues to make sentences.**

Changes in our town:

There is a new shopping centre.

Good things:

1 It / big / old shopping centre

It is bigger than the old shopping centre.

2 It / exciting / old shopping centre

_____

3 It / modern / old shopping centre

_____

Bad things:

4 It / busy / old shopping centre

_____

5 It / expensive / old shopping centre

_____

6 It / noisy / old shopping centre

_____

There is a new restaurant,

Good things:

7 The seats / comfortable / in the old restaurant

_____

8 The people / friendly / in the old restaurant

_____

9 The coffee / good / in the old restaurant

_____

Bad things:

10 The food / bad / in the old restaurant

_____

11 The rooms / dark / in the old restaurant

_____

12 The pizzas / small / in the old restaurant

_____

Grammar Alive Comparing places

5 *** **Use the information to make sentences comparing the Multi-Screen Cinema and the Royal Cinema. Use the correct form of the words below.**

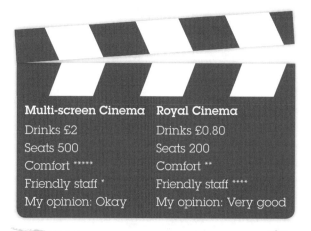

Multi-screen Cinema
Drinks £2
Seats 500
Comfort *****
Friendly staff *
My opinion: Okay

Royal Cinema
Drinks £0.80
Seats 200
Comfort **
Friendly staff ****
My opinion: Very good

bad   big   cheap   comfortable (less)   expensive
friendly (less)   good   small

1 Drinks in the Multi-screen cinema
are more expensive than drinks in the
Royal Cinema.

2 Drinks in the Royal Cinema

_____ .

3 The Multi-screen Cinema

_____ .

4 The Royal Cinema

_____ .

5 The seats in the Royal Cinema

_____ .

6 The seats in the Multi-screen Cinema

_____ .

7 The people who work in the Multi-screen Cinema

_____ .

8 The people who work in the Royal Cinema

_____ .

9 In my opinion, the Royal Cinema

_____ .

10 In my opinion, the Multi-screen Cinema

_____ .

SKILLS
Reading

1 Read the text and put the places in the correct column.

Plaza Mayor   Museo del Prado
The Louvre   Musee Carnavalet
The Pantheon   The Vatican Museum
The Place Georges Pompidou

Always free	Free on some days	Free at some times of the day
Plaza Mayor	_____	_____
_____	_____	
_____		

HOME   TRAVEL   BLOG   CONTACT US

Europe for free?

Europe is sometimes expensive but you can see and do some things for free!

PLAZA MAYOR in Madrid is very beautiful and you can walk around for free. The Museo del Prado in Madrid is free after six o'clock in the evening. It closes at eight so you can have two hours to look at some of the seven thousand paintings in the gallery.

THE LOUVRE in Paris is usually quite expensive but, on the first Sunday of every month it is free to enter. On other days, try the Musee Carnavalet where you can learn about the history of Paris – it is always free. The Place Georges Pompidou is also free – you can watch street performers and listen to musicians there.

ROME has got lots of free attractions like the two thousand year old Pantheon. Go to Piazza Navona and then walk to this beautiful Roman building. On the last Sunday of every month, the Vatican Museum is also free. The Settimana della Cultura is a week in April when Italy's national museums and galleries are all free to enter ... and very, very busy!

Don't stay at home. See Europe – for free – now!

2 Read the text again and complete the information.

Museo del Prado:
City: [1] _Madrid_
Free every day after: [2] _____
Closes at: [3] _____
Number of paintings: [4] _____

The Louvre:
Free on: [5] _____

Musee Carnavalet:
A good place to learn about [6] _____

Pantheon:
[7] _____ years old

Vatican Museum:
Free on: [8] _____

Settimana della Cultura:
A week in [9] _____ when all national museums and galleries in Italy are free

Word Builder Verbs and prepositions

3 Complete the sentences with the correct words.

1 Why stay _____at_____ home when there are so many places you can visit?
2 You can listen _____ musicians in Paris.
3 Don't go _____ the Louvre today. It's free tomorrow.
4 We can walk _____ the Trevi Fountain from here. It isn't far.
5 Look _____ all these paintings.
6 There's a tourist bus that goes _____ Rome and stops at all the famous sights but it is very expensive.
7 Lots of tourists come _____ my city every year.
8 Who lives _____ that palace over there?

Listening

4 **16** **Listen to someone talking about some free places to visit in New York (1-6). Match them with the things you do or can see there (a-f).**

1 Central Park _____d_____

2 The Guggenheim Museum _____

3 The Brooklyn Academy of Music _____

4 Brooklyn Botanical Garden _____

5 Bronx Zoo _____

6 The Staten Island Ferry _____

a Concerts

b A great view of Manhattan and the Statue of Liberty

c Beautiful plants

d Shakespeare's plays

e Animals

f Paintings by Picasso

5 **16** **Listen again and complete the information with one word, a number or a time.**

Shakespeare in the Park
There are free plays in the ¹___summer___ .
They are usually in the evening.

The Guggenheim Museum
You can 'pay what you want'
after ²_____ on ³_____ .

The Brooklyn Academy of Music
There are free concerts on ⁴_____
and ⁵_____ in the evening.

Brooklyn Botanical Garden
Free all day on ⁶_____ . Also free
for two hours on a ⁷_____ starting
at ⁸_____ .

Bronx Zoo
It is free every ⁹_____ .

Staten Island Ferry
It goes between Manhattan and Staten
Island ¹⁰_____ days a year and
travels all day and all night.

Sentence Builder Time prepositions

6 **Put the phrases below in the correct column.**

the morning   Saturdays   night   the weekend
the summer   Friday mornings   eight o'clock
the evening   Tuesday afternoons   Sunday evenings
the winter   half-past five

In	At	On
the morning	_____	_____
_____	_____	_____
_____	_____	_____
_____	_____	_____

7 **Choose the correct words to complete the sentences.**

1 There are concerts *in/at/on* the evenings and at *the summer/weekends/Fridays*.

2 You can sit at outside cafés in the *weekend/summer/Saturday afternoons*.

3 The museum opens *in/on/at* ten o'clock in *Mondays/the morning/the weekend* and closes at *the evening/seven o'clock/the afternoon*.

4 *In/On/At* Saturdays, the park opens from ten o'clock until six o'clock but, in *Sundays/the winter/Sunday mornings* it is sometimes closed.

5 A lot of people go out at *the evening/the summer/night*. The streets are always busy, even *in/at/on* five o'clock *in/at/on* the morning.

GRAMMAR
Superlatives

1 * **Complete the text with the correct form of the adjectives in brackets.**

One of the ¹___nicest___ (nice) cities I know is Olomouc in the Czech Republic. The ²_____ (good) thing about the city is that there aren't many tourists. The ³_____ (busy) times are when people go to work and come home again. The ⁴_____ (famous) place in the Czech Republic is Prague. It is the ⁵_____ (big) city and it is where most people go to. Olomouc is one of the ⁶_____ (difficult) places to get to from Prague so people visit other towns and cities nearer to Prague. That's why it's one of the ⁷_____ (quiet) cities in the country. What's the ⁸_____ (bad) thing about it? It's one of the ⁹_____ (expensive) cities in the country.

2 * **Complete the sentences with *most* or *least*.**

1 The ___most___ famous painting in the Louvre is the Mona Lisa.
2 The _____ expensive places to stay are not always the worst places to stay.
3 The _____ exciting town in England is my town. Nothing ever happens here.
4 The _____ expensive pizza is €50. Let's eat a cheaper one!
5 The _____ exciting place I know is Disney World in Orlando. It's great!
6 Don't go to the park at night. It's the _____ dangerous part of the city.

3 ** **Complete the dialogue using superlative forms.**

Adam: Where do you want to go this summer? Greece, Poland or Italy?
Kate: Well ¹Poland / cheap
___Poland is the cheapest___ of the three countries
Adam: Yes, but I like Italy.
Kate: ²Italy / expensive _____
of the three. Poland's better.
Adam: But the people in Italy are really friendly.
Kate: I think ³friendly / people _____
are the Greeks.
Adam: That's true. And ⁴Greece / relaxing
_____ of the three countries.
Kate: So, let's go to Greece.
Adam: But Italy ⁵has / nice / food _____
of the three countries.
Kate: Oh yes. Pizza! But ⁶Italy / noisy
_____ country.
Adam: It's very difficult. Which ⁷good
_____ country to go to?

Grammar Alive Talking about cities

4 *** **Use the cues to complete the dialogues.**

1 **A:** Warsaw / big / city in Poland
   B: Yes, but Krakow / interesting / Polish city
   A: *Warsaw is the biggest city in Poland.*
   B: *Yes, but Krakow is the most interesting Polish city.*

2 **A:** Rome / famous / city in Italy
   B: Yes, but Venice / beautiful / Italian city
   A: _____
   B: _____

3 **A:** New York / busy / city in the USA
   B: Yes, and it / cool / city in the world
   A: _____
   B: _____

4 **A:** Athens / dangerous / city in Greece
   B: Yes, but Greece / one of / safe / countries in Europe
   A: _____
   B: _____

5 **A:** Canberra / one of / modern / cities in Australia
   B: Yes, but / boring / city in the country
   A: _____
   B: _____

6 **A:** London / exciting / city in Britain
   B: Yes, but it / expensive / city in the country
   A: _____
   B: _____

Speaking Workshop 3

❶ Choose the correct words to complete the questions.

1 Can we _b_ some information about the festival, please?

   a give   **b** have   **c** do

2 When ___ it start?

   a is   **b** has   **c** does

3 How ___ are the tickets?

   a much   **b** cost   **c** many

4 What shows ___ ?

   a there   **b** are there   **c** there are

5 Where ___ the festival?

   a is   **b** does   **c** has

6 What ___ things can we see there?

   a much   **b** kind   **c** other

❷ Match the answers (a-e) with the questions in Exercise 1. There is one question with no answer.

a There are a lot of other things to see and do.   _6_

b In Manor Park.   ___

c It's free. There aren't any tickets.   ___

d On Friday evening and it finishes on Sunday evening.   ___

e It's a music festival. You can listen to rap, pop, rock and other things.   ___

❸ Which answer doesn't match the questions?

1 Can we have some information about the film, please?

   a Of course.

   b What do you want to know?

   c You're welcome.

2 What kind of music do they play?

   a Pop

   b Horror

   c Rap

3 How much are the tickets?

   a They're free.

   b There are 450 tickets.

   c £5

4 When does it start?

   a On Saturday morning.

   b At five o'clock.

   c At the theatre.

5 Where is the festival?

   a There are some comedy shows.

   b At the theatre.

   c In the park.

❹ 17 Complete the dialogue with the phrases below. Then listen to check.

In the City, near London Bridge.
~~Hi. Can I help you?~~ You're welcome!
The tickets cost from thirty five to fifty pounds.
Of course. Well, there is a big rock concert on Saturday - with five groups.
Sure. There's a comedy and music night this Friday. It's very funny. Billy Baker and his Band. They're the best.

Zac: ¹_Hi. Can I help you?_____

Patsy: Yes, can we have some information about concerts and shows for this weekend, please?

Zac: ²_____

Patsy: Perfect! What kind of music do they play?

Gary: How much are the tickets?

Zac: ³_____

Patsy: Fifty pounds?

Gary: Are there any cheaper shows?

Zac: ⁴_____

...

Gary: Excuse me. Where is this festival?

Zac: ⁵_____

Gary: What time does it start?

Patsy: Friday at seven!

Gary: That's tonight! Let's do it! Thanks for all your help.

Zac: ⁶_____

Writing Workshop 2

1 Complete the emails with the phrases (a–e) in the gaps (1–5).

- **a** at my place
- **b** Thanks for
- **c** What are you up to
- **d** Call me.
- **e** Do you fancy going

From:	Ben
To:	Tom

Hi Tom,
¹ _c_ next Saturday? ² ___ to a concert with me? My brother's got a ticket ªand/but he can't go now. They are only £5 and there are some great bands there.
³ ___
Ben

From:	Tom
To:	Ben

Hi Ben,
⁴ ___ the message. I want to go ᵇand/but I haven't got much money. Can your brother wait for the £5?
Tom

From:	Tom
To:	Ben

Tom
Of course. No problem. Why don't we meet ⁵ ___ in the afternoon ᶜand/but play some computer games before we go? My dad can collect us from the concert ᵈand/but he can't take us.
Ben

From:	Ben
To:	Tom

Ben
Okay. Don't worry. There are a lot of buses on Saturday.
See you at about three o'clock.
Tom

2 Choose the correct words (a–d) to complete the emails in Exercise 1.

3 Complete the sentences with *and* or *but*.

1 I like films ___ _but_ ___ I don't like going to the cinema.
2 Tickets are free _____ food and drink at the festival are very expensive.
3 I meet my friends on Saturdays _____ we go shopping together.
4 I want to go to the concert _____ I haven't got any time.
5 There are a lot of buses to the town centre _____ tickets are very cheap.
6 The group play rap _____ rock _____ they don't play pop.

4 Use the cues to write a message and a reply.

Hi Gemma,
1 what / up to / Friday evening?
   What are you up to on Friday evening?
2 there is / comedy show / theatre
   _____
3 tickets / only £2
   _____
4 fancy / go?
   _____
5 call
   _____
Natalie

Hi Natalie,
6 thanks / message
   _____
7 Yes, that / great idea
   _____
8 Why / we meet / my place?
   _____
9 can walk / theatre
   _____
10 see / about six o'clock / Friday
   _____
Gemma

Sound Choice 2

Sound Check

Say the words and expressions below.

a bigger, nicest, longer (Exercise 1)

b bathroom, Thursday, maths (Exercise 2)

c he's, his, cheap (Exercise 3)

d cheap, street, read (Exercise 4)

e Why don't we play a video game? How much are the tickets? (Exercise 5)

f outdoor, art, theatre (Exercise 6)

18 **Listen and check your answers. Which sounds and expressions did you have problems with? Choose three exercises to do below.**

1 **19** Grammar **Listen and repeat the words.**

1 big - bigger
2 nice - nicest
3 long - longer
4 busy - busiest
5 old - older
6 small - smallest

2 **20** Consonants - Unstressed schwa sound **Listen and repeat the words.**

1 bathroom
2 birthday
3 thirsty
4 theatre
5 Thursday
6 maths

3 **21** Vowels - /ɪ/ and /iː/ **Listen to the words. Which vowel sound do they have, /ɪ/ or /iː/?**

1 he's   /iː/
2 his   ___
3 this   ___
4 these   ___
5 cheap   ___
6 big   ___
7 sleep   ___
8 machine   ___

4 **22** Spelling **Listen and decide whether the word is spelt with *ea* or *ee*.**

1 *ea*
2 ___
3 ___
4 ___
5 ___
6 ___
7 ___
8 ___

5 **23** Expressions **Listen and repeat the expressions.**

1 Why don't we play a video game?
2 How much are the tickets?
3 Let's go home.
4 Good idea.
5 What kind of music do they play?
6 What time does it start?

6 **24** **Listen to the words and write them. Underline the silent *r*.**

1 *outdoor*
2 _____
3 _____
4 _____
5 _____
6 _____
7 _____
8 _____
9 _____

Check Your Progress 3

1 Places **Complete the words.**

1 I love the food at the new Italian
r _ _ _ _ _ r _ _ _ .

2 We go dancing at a n_ _ _ _ c_ _ _ on Fridays.

3 There are a lot of different shops in the new
s_ _ _ _ _ _ _ c _ _ t _ _ .

4 The clothes in the o_ _ d_ _ _ _ m _ _ k_ _
are cheaper than in the shops.

5 You can see an exhibition of paintings by Renoir at
our local a_ _ g _ _ _ _ r _

6 I like going to see films at the c_ _ _ _ _ _ .

7 We can swim at the s_ _ _ _ _ _ _ _ p_ _ _ .

8 I play basketball at the s_ _ r_ _ c_ _ t _ _ .

/8

2 Adjectives **Match the adjectives with the
sentences. There are three extra adjectives.**

boring   busy   cheap   comfortable   dark
expensive   friendly   noisy   quiet

1 In our museum, people don't talk. They look at
the objects and don't say anything. _____

2 There's nothing to do here. _____

3 How much?? €50 for a T-shirt! _____

4 I love these armchairs. You can sleep in them, they
are so nice. _____

5 There are always a lot of people in the skate park.
Sometimes you can't move. _____

6 The people in the market always say *Hello*.
_____

/6

3 Comparatives **Use the cues to make sentences.**

1 The shopping centre / big / the market
_____

2 The market / interesting / the shopping centre
_____

3 The market / cheap / the shopping centre
_____

4 The shopping centre / busy / the market
_____

5 The park / relaxing / the amusement park
_____

6 The amusement park / noisy / the park
_____

7 The amusement park / exciting / the park
_____

8 The park / good / the amusement park for children
_____

/8

4 Verbs and prepositions / Time prepositions
Complete the sentences with the correct words.

1 I stay _____ home _____ Sundays.

2 Come _____ my house _____ the weekend.

3 We live _____ that house _____ the summer.

4 I always listen _____ the radio _____ five o'clock.

/8

5 Superlatives **Look at the information and use the
cues to make sentences with *most* and *least*.**

	Sky Amusement Park	Fun City Amusement Park	Wild Amusement Park
Ticket	£10	£20	£25
People	2000 a day	1000 a day	5000 a day
My opinion	Boring	Very exciting	Okay.

1 Sky Amusement Park / expensive
_____ amusement park.

2 Fun City Amusement Park / busy
_____ amusement park.

3 Fun City Amusement Park / exciting
_____ amusement park.

4 Sky Amusement Park / exciting
_____ amusement park in Devon.

5 Wild Amusement Park / expensive
_____ amusement park in Devon.

/5

TOTAL SCORE   **/35**

Module Diary 3

1 **Look at the objectives on page 31 in the
Students' Book. Choose three and evaluate
your learning.**

1 Now I can _____ well / quite well /
with problems.

2 Now I can _____ well / quite well /
with problems.

3 Now I can _____ well / quite well /
with problems.

2 **Look at your results. What language areas
in this module do you need to study more?**

TOPIC TALK – VOCABULARY

1 Write the dates in words. Use the months below.

April   August   December   February   January   ~~July~~
November

1	5/7	The _fifth of July._
2	21/12	The _____
3	15/4	The _____
4	30/11	The _____
5	8/8	The _____
6	11/1	The _____
7	12/2	The _____

2 Choose the correct way to say the years.

1 2007
  (a) two thousand and seven
  b twenty o seven
  c two thousand zero zero seven

2 1999
  a one thousand nine hundred and ninety-nine
  b Nineteen ninety-nine
  c Nineteen hundred and ninety-nine

3 2012
  a twenty hundred and twelve
  b twenty twelve
  c twenty one two

4 2000
  a twenty o o
  b twenty hundred
  c two thousand

5 1990
  a nineteen ninety
  b ninety nineteen
  c one thousand nine hundred and ninety

3 Replace the underlined words with the phrases below. There are two extra phrases.

four years ago   last month   last summer
last year   five months ago   ~~three years ago~~
two months ago

July 1756

1 I started planning this journey to America <u>in 1753</u>.
  Three years ago.

2 We left England <u>in 1755</u>.
  _____

3 We arrived in Spain in the <u>summer of 1755</u>.
  _____

4 We arrived in America <u>in February 1756</u>.
  _____

5 We left America <u>in June 1756</u>.
  _____

4 Match the beginnings (1-7) with the correct endings (a-g). Then write the numbers in words.

1 My birthday is _d_
2 My earliest birthday memory ___
3 My best birthday ever ___
4 On my 9th _____ birthday we had a party on ___
5 On my sister's 16th _____ birthday, she had a picnic in ___
6 On my mum's 40th _____ birthday, we had lunch at ___
7 I always have parties with ___

a was my 13th _____ birthday in 2006 _____ .
b the beach.
c a restaurant.
d on 15/10 _the fifteenth of October._
e was my 4th _____ birthday.
f my friends.
g the country.

10

Past Simple

1 * **Complete the text with *was* or *were*.**

I remember my old school very well. I remember Mr Smith. He ¹____*was*____ very kind. Most of our teachers ²_____ old but he ³_____ young.
It ⁴_____ an old school. The rooms ⁵_____ big and cold. The chairs ⁶_____ uncomfortable and the desks ⁷_____ small. Our room ⁸_____ very dark. The photos on the walls ⁹_____ black and white and the windows ¹⁰_____ small. My new school is much nicer.

2 * **Complete the text with the past form of the verbs in brackets.**

When I was young, I had a cat. I ¹____*called*____ (call) her Pickles and I always ²_____ (want) to take her to school with me. I often ³_____ (ask) my parents but they always said 'No!'. Then, one day, we had a 'pet day' at school. I took Pickles on the bus. She ⁴_____ (hate) it! At school, we all ⁵_____ (show) our pets to the class and ⁶_____ (talk) about them. One boy had a big dog. The dog got onto the teacher's desk and ⁷_____ (stay) there. We all ⁸_____ (laugh) but I think our teacher was scared!

3 ** **Complete the sentences with the past form of the verbs below.**

buy   do   eat   ~~go~~   have   know   leave   send

Last year I …
1 ____*went*____ to school by bus every day.
2 _____ long hair.
3 _____ my phone on the bus and lost it.
4 _____ lots of computer games from a shop in the town centre.
5 _____ my homework every day.
6 _____ pizza every Friday.
7 _____ emails to my friends every day.
8 only _____ twenty German words.

4 ** **Complete the sentences with the correct form of *was* or *were*.**

1 My parents __*weren't bad*__ (not bad) students, they __*were good*__ (good) students.
2 I _____ (not bored) in the lesson, I _____ (tired).
3 Our old French teacher (not strict) _____ . He _____ (friendly).
4 That book _____ (not interesting). It _____ (boring).
5 The shops _____ (not open) when we got to the town centre. They _____ (closed).
6 I _____ (not serious) about my school work when I was young. I _____ (very relaxed)!
7 I looked for my phone in my bag but it _____ (not there). It _____ (on) my desk.
8 It _____ (not cold) yesterday, it _____ (hot).

5 ** **Complete the sentences with the negative forms of the verbs in brackets.**

1 Last year, I __*didn't like*__ (not like) English.
2 I _____ (not use) my computer yesterday.
3 We _____ (not go) swimming last Saturday.
4 Last summer, my dad _____ (not have) a holiday.
5 My sister _____ (not invite) me to her birthday party!
6 I _____ (not want) to have tennis lessons but now I like them.
7 My friend _____ (not do) his homework yesterday.
8 I went to a party but I _____ (not know) any of the people there.

6 *** Complete the text with the words below.

> didn't (x 2)   go   had (x 2)   have   saw   stayed
> was (x 2)   wasn't   went (x̶ ̶2̶)   were (x 2)   weren't

Last month, we ¹___*went*___ on a school
trip to France. We ²_____ a great
time. I ³_____ speak much French. We
⁴_____ lessons in the morning but we didn't
⁵_____ any homework to do.
We ⁶_____ in a small town about fifty
kilometres from Paris. It ⁷_____ a very
quiet town. The cinema ⁸_____ open so
we ⁹_____ watch any films. The shops
¹⁰_____ very big – they ¹¹_____
much smaller than the shops in our town. We didn't
¹²_____ out in the evening at all but I liked
the town. The people ¹³_____ very friendly
and the food ¹⁴_____ great!
On the last day, we ¹⁵_____ to Paris and
¹⁶_____ the Eiffel Tower. I love Paris!

7 *** Make sentences from the cues.

Last year, I went to Italy.

1 ✓ see / the Coliseum
   *I saw the Coliseum.*_____

2 ✗ / go inside
   _____

3 ✓ / eat / real Italian pizza
   _____

4 ✗ / like it
   _____

5 ✓ / go to an art gallery
   _____

6 ✗ / see / any paintings by Leonardo Da Vinci
   _____

7 ✗ / write / to my friends
   _____

8 ✓ / send / them emails
   _____

Grammar Alive Excuses

8 *** Use the cues to make dialogues.

1 A: You not / send me / email yesterday
   B: I / have / lot / homework to do
   A: *You didn't send me an email yesterday.*
   B: *I had a lot of homework to do.*

2 A: You / use / my phone. You / not ask me
   B: You / not be here. I / only talk / for one minute
   A: _____
   B: _____

3 A: You laugh / my hair
   B: I / not want / laugh. Sorry
   A: _____
   B: _____

4 A: You / be / late for school yesterday
   B: I / go / by bus. It / be / late
   A: _____
   B: _____

5 A: You / not say / hello to me yesterday
   B: Sorry. I / not see / you
   A: _____
   B: _____

❶ Read Paul's story. Match the headings (1-5) with the correct paragraphs (A-D). There is one extra heading.

1 Finding lost family
2 Problems at home
3 A sad start
4 Family visits
5 Granddad's family

A _3_ My grandfather and his sister were born in 1942. When they were three months old, their mum died. Their dad was in Egypt with the army and they didn't have any grandparents. My grandfather went to live with a family in London. His sister went to live with a family in Australia.

B ___ My grandfather was a happy child and liked his family. He was always sad that he didn't have any brothers or sister. He didn't know he had a sister in Australia. He got married in 1963 and he and my grandmother had three children; my dad, Mark, his brother, Rob, and his sister, Louisa.

C ___ Later, my grandfather's parents told him about his real family and his sister, Helen. In 2002, my father started looking for her on the internet. Then, in 2004, he found her. She was in Melbourne and she had three children called … Mark, Rob and Louisa!

D ___ Dad wrote to her and she invited us to Australia. We went in 2010. My grandfather was nervous but we had a great time. The next year, Helen came to England with six of her grandchildren! I've now got a much bigger family than I had two years ago!

❷ Read the text again. Are the sentences true (T) or false (F)?

1 Paul's grandfather is a year older than his sister. _F_
2 His grandfather lived with his real father after the war. ___
3 His grandfather was sad when he was young because his sister was in Australia. ___
4 Paul's father has got one brother and one sister. ___
5 Helen is the writer's grandmother. ___
6 Helen's children have got the same names as the writer's grandfather's children. ___
7 The writer and his grandfather first met Helen in Australia. ___

Word Builder Adverbs

❸ Choose the word which is *wrong* in each sentence.

1 You drive very _b_ .
  a fast   b quick   c slowly
2 Jason sings very ___ .
  a well   b badly   c good
3 The children played ___ .
  a noisy   b happily   c quietly
4 She always works ___ .
  a hard   b well   c hardly
5 I looked at my friend's photos ___ .
  a sadly   b slow   c quickly

❹ Complete the sentences with the adjective in brackets and an adverb made from the adjective in the correct places.

1 I ran ___*quickly*___ . I'm a very ___*quick*___ runner. (quick)
2 You did _____ in your exam. You're a very _____ student. (good)
3 The children were very _____ . They worked, played and ate _____ . (happy)
4 Your brother is a _____ worker. He always works _____ . (hard)
5 Mum and Dad were _____ when I got home. They shouted at me _____ . (angry)

Sentence Builder Time linkers

5 **Choose the correct words to complete the sentences.**

1 I was at home *when*/*then* I saw the news on TV.
2 *Before/After* I went to sleep, I read for half an hour.
3 My dad left school when he was sixteen. He *after/then* joined the army.
4 *Then/After* I did my homework, I played some computer games.
5 I met my friends at the café *and/after* then we went shopping.

6 **Complete the sentences with the time linkers below.**

when   then   after   ~~before~~   and

1 ___Before___ we left the cinema, I went home. It rained all day and we didn't know what to do. First of all we went to an art gallery. We ²_____ visited a museum ³_____ then went shopping in the shopping centre.
My dad is a teacher. He started teaching when he was thirty. ⁴_____ that, he worked in a restaurant. We were in an exam ⁵_____ my phone rang. The teacher was very angry.

7 **Put the story into the correct order.**

a I was at a concert when I met Tom.   _1_
b We didn't talk because the music was very loud. After the concert, we walked to the bus stop.   ___
c We talked for a few minutes and then my bus came and we said goodbye.   ___
d It was on July 20, the first day of the school holidays. It was about nine o'clock when Tom sat next to me and asked me for the time.   ___
e Tom asked me for my phone number and I wrote it on a piece of paper.   ___
f I got my phone out and showed him the time on that. He started talking about the phone and then the band started.   ___

8 **Match the notes (1-7) with the questions (a-g).**

1 Where did they meet?   _c_
2 When did they meet?   ___
3 Describe her appearance   ___
4 What happened first?   ___
5 Then what did Jack say?   ___
6 How did he feel?   ___
7 What happened at the end of the meeting?   ___

a long blond hair, blue eyes, slim, tall, nice smile
b excited, happy
c at a party
d He smiled at her and sat next to her.
e They said goodbye, asked for her phone number, agreed to meet again.
f He asked her to dance.
g last Saturday

9 **Use the ideas in Exercise 8 to write about a meeting between Jack and Emma.**

Jack and Emma met …

GRAMMAR
Past Simple: questions

❶ * Make questions from the sentences.

1 You were tired.
Were you tired?

2 She was tall.
_____ tall?

3 Your keys were in your bag.
_____ in your bag?

4 My dad was angry.
_____ angry?

5 The film was interesting.
_____ interesting?

6 Their party was in June.
_____ in June?

7 Your teachers were very strict.
_____ very strict?

8 Your brother's friend was hungry.
_____ hungry?

❷ ** Complete the questions with the words in brackets.

1 Where *did you go* last weekend? (you / go)

2 Who _____ to at the party? (you / talk)

3 What _____ in the shops? (she / buy)

4 How _____ back home after the film? (they / get)

5 _____ the football match? (your dad / see)

6 What _____ on your birthday? (you / do)

7 How many presents _____ for her birthday? (Helen / get)

8 Why _____ Paul to his party? (Tom / invite)

❸ *** Complete the questions for the answers.

1 What film *did you go to see?*
We went to see *Midnight in Paris*.

2 _____ last night?
Yes, I was. I was very hungry.

3 How many people _____ ?
I invited about twenty people to my party.

4 What time _____ ?
They got back home at about eleven o'clock.

5 Where _____ on Sunday?
My parents were at a restaurant on Sunday.

6 _____ any homework yesterday?
Yes, he did. Our English teacher always gives us homework.

Grammar Alive Questioning

❹ *** Use the cues to make questions and answers.

1 A: What time / you / get up?
B: I / half past seven
What time did you get up?
I got up at half-past seven.

2 A: What / eat / for breakfast?
B: not eat / any breakfast
_____
_____

3 A: Where / you / ten o'clock?
B: I / be / at school
_____
_____

4 A: you / have / an exam yesterday?
B: Yes, we /. We / have / English exam
_____
_____

5 A: it easy?
B: No, / not
_____
_____

6 A: What / do / evening?
B: watch / a film on TV
_____
_____

Speaking Workshop 4

Talk Builder Talking about memories

1 Match the beginnings (1–8) with the correct endings (a–h).

1 Do you remember   _e_
2 Oh yes, I remember   ___
3 And after you found it   ___
4 Do you remember the girl   ___
5 Yes, but I don't   ___
6 I do. I remember we finished our pizzas and ___
7 And we were at the bus stop   ___
8 And after   ___

a remember her name.
b we went for a pizza.
c when the girl came up to us and gave you your phone.
d that, I went back to the pizza restaurant every day to try to find her again!
e when you lost your phone?
f at the next table?
g then got up and left.
h that.

2 Choose the correct words to complete the sentences.

1 **A:** Do you remember _c_ we went on a school trip to the museum?
   a then   **b** after   **c** when
  B: Yes, and after ___ Mr Finch bought us all a drink in the museum café.
   a that   **b** when   **c** then

2 **A:** Do you remember ___ really long game of tennis we had?
   a this   **b** that   **c** when
  B: No, I don't remember ___ .
   a him   **b** this   **c** that

3 **A:** We watched this film last week.
  B: Did we?
  A: Yes. You don't remember ___ you were asleep.
   a but   **b** because   **c** when
  B: Oh yes.
  A: And ___ you woke up, you wanted to go dancing.
   a then   **b** after that   **c** when
  B: That's right.
  A: And ___ you asked us why we were so tired!
   a when   **b** then   **c** because

3 Complete the dialogue with the correct words.

Paula: Do you [1] _remember_ my birthday last year?
Nikki: Yes, I remember [2] _____ . It was a great party.
Paula: We went into the garden and started singing.
Nikki: I don't remember [3] _____ .
Paula: You don't remember [4] _____ you were in the living room with Will.
Nikki: Yes. He came and talked to me and [5] _____ he asked me to dance.
Paula: And [6] _____ that he asked you to go to the cinema.
Nikki: Yes, and he's still my boyfriend.

4 **25** Use the cues to complete the dialogues. Then listen to check.

1 **A:** remember / our class / have a picnic on the beach?
  B: No, / not / remember / that
  A: You / not / remember because / you not be / there
  B: Oh yes. I / be really sad / you tell / me about it the next day
  A: _Do you remember when our class had a_ _picnic on the beach?_
  B: _____
  A: _____
  B: _____

2 **A:** remember / I buy / this CD
  B: Yes / remember / that
  B: You / not have / any money
  B: I / give / £10
  A: I / not remember
  B: I know!
  A: _____
  B: _____
  B: _____
  B: _____
  A: _____
  B: I know!

Exam Choice 2

Reading

1 Read the text. Match the headings (1–5) with the paragraphs (a–d). There is one extra heading.

1 Things to do
2 Size
3 Money
4 Where it is
5 Opening Times

20th April

Pyramid Shopping Centre

A ___ The new shopping centre is much bigger and better than the old one. There are 240 shops in the centre. The old centre had 110.

B ___ You can visit the new centre more often. The old centre was open from nine in the morning until five in the evening from Monday to Saturday but was closed on Sundays. The new centre is open from eight in the morning and closes at ten o'clock in the evening. That's every day of the week, Monday to Sunday.

C ___ The new centre isn't just for shopping. There are a lot of nice places to eat and drink in the new centre. There are four restaurants and seven cafés. The old centre had only one café and it wasn't very nice. There is also a cinema, a children's play area and a small art gallery at the new centre.

D ___ Some people say that the old shopping centre was cheaper but that's not true! We bought ten things from different shops in the old centre and spent £85.43. We bought the same ten things at the new centre and spent only £74.65.

---

2 Read the text again and complete the information.

	The Pyramid Shopping Centre	The old centre
Number of shops:	1 _____	2 _____
Opening times: Monday – Saturday	3 _____	4 _____
Sunday	5 _____	6 _____
Number of restaurants:	7 _____	None
Number of cafés:	8 _____	9 _____
Other places to go:	10 _____	

Listening

3 🔊 26 Listen to a message from a language school and complete the information.

Name of school: Big [1]_____
Date courses start: [2]_____
Days lessons are on: [3]_____ and
[4]_____

Times of lessons:
Beginners [5]_____ – 5.00
Elementary 5.15 – [6]_____
Advanced 7.00 – 8.30
Price of lessons: [7]_____ a month.
(£40 for students at the school last year)
School opens at: [8]_____
On Saturdays, the school is open from: 10.00 – [9]_____

Speaking

4 Complete the dialogue with the correct words. You can see the first letter of each word.

Emily: There's a concert on Saturday. Do you want to go?
Victoria: I don't know. [1]W_____ is it?
Emily: At the theatre.
Victoria: [2]H_____ m_____ are the tickets?
Emily: I think they're about £10.
Victoria: That's not bad. What [3]t_____ d_____ it s_____ ?
Emily: It starts at seven o'clock. There are three bands and it finishes at about ten o'clock.
Victoria: What [4]k_____ of music do they play?
Emily: Rock and rap.
Victoria: Great. What are the bands called?
Emily: I don't [5]r_____ their names. Sorry.
Victoria: Okay. Let's go to the theatre and buy two tickets and [6]t_____ we can go shopping.
Emily: Great and [7]a_____ that we can have a pizza.
Victoria: Good idea.

Use of English

5 Read the descriptions and write the places.

1 We sometimes go there for dinner.

r_ _ _ _ _ _ _ _ _

2 My sister goes there every Friday to dance.

n_ _ _ _ _ c_ _ _ _

3 People like to go there for a drink and to meet friends.

p_ _ _

4 You can see some great paintings there.

a_ _ g_ _ _ _ _ _ _

5 You can learn about local history here.

m_ _ _ _ _ _

6 We go here with our skateboards.

s_ _ _ _ _ p_ _ _

7 It's a nice place to go shopping – in the summer.

o_ _ _ _ _ _ m_ _ _ _ _

6 Choose the correct words to complete the sentences.

1 English lessons are ___ interesting than playing sports.

  a most   **b** better   **c** more

2 My birthday is on the fifth ___ November.

  a in   **b** of   **c** day

3 We went to Spain ___ summer.

  a last   **b** past   **c** in

4 Where ___ you yesterday?

  a did   **b** was   **c** were

5 I did very ___ in my exams.

  a good   **b** bad   **c** well

6 Who ___ you invite to your party?

  a did   **b** were   **c** was

7 We went to America two years ___ .

  a past   **b** away   **c** ago

8 This is the ___ game I've got.

  a best   **b** better   **c** most

Writing

7 Match the beginnings (1-7) with the correct endings (a-g).

1 What are you doing   ___

2 Do you fancy   ___

3 Why don't we meet at my   ___

4 Call   ___

5 Thanks   ___

6 We can meet at my house and   ___

7 I like swimming but   ___

a I haven't got time this weekend.

b place?

c go by bus.

d at the weekend?

e me.

f going swimming?

g for the invitation.

8 Write a short message to a friend suggesting meeting at the weekend.

- Ask your friend what he/she is doing and make your suggestion
- Tell your friend where/when the activity takes place and how much the tickets are.
- Suggest a place and time to meet

What are you doing ... ?

Check Your Progress 4

1 Birthday memories **Complete the dates with the correct words.**

1 24/1/1990 The twenty-fourth of _____ , nineteen ninety.
2 31/3/2001 The thirty-first of March, two _____ and one.
3 2/10 The _____ of October.
4 3/8 The _____ of August.
5 11/9 The eleventh of _____ .
6 10/5/2010 The _____ of May, two thousand and ten.
7 20/6/1968 The _____ of June nineteen sixty-eight.
8 12/12 The _____ of December.

/8

2 Past Simple **Complete the sentences with the correct form of the verbs in brackets.**

1 I _____ (not be) very happy yesterday.
2 I _____ (buy) a concert ticket yesterday.
3 Cathy _____ (not know) about the exam and she did very badly.
4 I went to the shop but I _____ (not have) any money.
5 It _____ (be) a great film.
6 I _____ (leave) my school bag at school.
7 Our teacher _____ (tell) us to be quiet.
8 The people in the café _____ (not be) friendly.

/8

3 Past simple questions **Use the cues to make questions and answers.**

1 **A:** you be in the bath when I / phone?
   B: No / not. I / be asleep

   _____

   _____

2 **A:** you / like the present I / give / you?
   B: Yes, I /. It / be / great

   _____

   _____

3 **A:** Where / you / go on holiday last year?
   B: We / go / to France. We / have / a great time

   _____

   _____

4 **A:** How many people / be / at the party last night?
   B: There / be / ten people. It / not be / a good party

   _____

   _____

/8

4 Adverbs **Complete the sentences with the correct adverbs. You can see the first letter of each word.**

1 Sharon works very h＿ ＿ ＿ and gets very good marks in all her exams.
2 Tom shouted a＿ ＿ ＿ ＿ ＿ ＿ at his friend because she took his MP3 player and didn't tell him.
3 We finished dinner very q＿ ＿ ＿ ＿ ＿ ＿ because we wanted to go to the cinema.
4 You play the guitar really w＿ ＿ ＿ . Do you want to be in our band?
5 The people at the football match sang n＿ ＿ ＿ ＿ ＿ ＿ and excitedly.

/5

5 Time linkers **Complete the dialogues with the words below.**

after   and   before   that   then   when

1 I played football _____ then had a shower.
2 _____ I got this book, I didn't like reading but now I love it.
3 I was at school _____ he first said 'Hello'.
4 When Sam was sixteen, he did badly in his exams. He _____ left school and got a job.
5 I first met Peter at a party. After _____ we became very good friends.
6 _____ the game of tennis I was really tired and hot. I had a long drink of water and felt better.

/6

TOTAL SCORE   /35

Module Diary 4

1 **Look at the objectives on page 39 in the Students' Book. Choose three and evaluate your learning.**

1 Now I can _____ well / quite well / with problems.
2 Now I can _____ well / quite well / with problems.
3 Now I can _____ well / quite well / with problems.

2 **Look at your results. What language areas in this module do you need to study more?**

TOPIC TALK – VOCABULARY

1 Look at the pictures and complete the activities.

	¹y	o	g	a					
²	x			c		s			
		³		t	l			c	
⁴				i					
			⁵v						
	⁶		i						
		⁷t							
	⁸		i						
⁹			e						
	¹⁰		s						

 1

 2

 3

 4

 5

 6

 7

 8

 9

 10

2 Complete the sentences with the correct form of *do* or *play*.

1 Do you often _____do_____ exercise?
2 My brother _____ rugby for the school team.
3 I like _____ tennis.
4 My friend _____ judo twice a week.
5 My mum _____ yoga at the new sports centre.
6 We _____ gymnastics at school yesterday.
7 My dad _____ football for the town team when he was younger.

3 Complete the sentences with the correct words. You can see the first letter of each word.

I usually ¹c_ycle_____ to school. I've got an old bike so I don't worry about it. Sometimes when it is raining, I go to school ²b _____ car. At the weekend, I usually go to my friend's house. He lives fifty metres away from me so I can ³w _____ there in one minute.

I often visit my grandparents. They live on the fourth floor. I usually ⁴t _____ the ⁵l _____ but sometimes it doesn't work and I ⁶w _____ ⁷u _____ the ⁸s _____ . It's good exercise!

4 Choose the correct word to complete the sentences.

1 I play basketball ___ a week on Mondays and Thursdays.
   a times   **b** two   **c** twice
2 I don't like rugby ___ I like hockey.
   a and   **b** but   **c** because
3 My sister likes table tennis ___ loves tennis.
   a but   **b** and   **c** or
4 My dad ___ goes to work by car, every day.
   a always   **b** never   **c** sometimes
5 I don't do much exercise so I'm not very ___ .
   a hard   **b** fit   **c** good
6 We go dancing ___ a week on Friday evenings.
   a one   **b** first   **c** once
7 My brother doesn't have much free time because he does judo three ___ a week.
   a goes   **b** turns   **c** times

13

Present Continuous

1 *** Write the *-ing* forms of the verbs.**

1 swim _____swimming_____
2 come _____
3 play _____
4 climb _____
5 run _____
6 dance _____
7 ride _____
8 ski _____
9 trek _____
10 cycle _____
11 walk _____
12 go _____

2 *** Complete the sentences with the correct form of the verbs in brackets.**

At the moment …
1 I _am watching_ (watch) television.
2 My brother _____ (read) a book.
3 My sister _____ (shop).
4 My parents _____ (work).
5 My grandfather _____ (play) tennis.
6 My grandmother _____ (listen) to the radio.
7 My friends _____ (buy) presents.
8 My dog _____ (sleep).

3 **** Complete the sentences with the correct form of the verbs below.**

buy ~~cycle~~ dance do listen
sleep walk watch

1 My brother ___is cycling___ on his new bike.
2 My sister _____ at a nightclub.
3 My mum _____ some food for dinner.
4 I _____ to music in my room.
5 My dad _____ in his bedroom because he worked all last night.
6 My friends _____ a film.
7 The students _____ their homework.
8 My friend and I _____ to school.

4 **** Write what is happening in the pictures using the verbs below in the correct form.**

cycle ~~dance~~ do drive play skateboard

1
They _are dancing._

2
He _____ judo

3
She _____

4
They _____ basketball

5
He _____

6
She _____

5 *** **Use the cues to write sentences.**

1 I / not watch / TV. I / do / my homework
I'm not watching TV. I'm doing my homework.

2 We / not do / an exam. We / work / in groups
_____

3 They / not play / tennis. They / play / volleyball
_____

4 She / not work. She / write / a letter
_____

5 He / not walk. He / sit / on the bus
_____

6 You / not study / for your exams. You / surf / the internet
_____

7 You / not listen / to me. You / look / out of the window
_____

6 *** **Complete the questions and short answers.**

1 **A:** *Are you using* (you use) your phone at the moment?
 B: ✓ *Yes, I am.*

2 **A:** _____ (your parents plan) their summer holidays at the moment?
 B: ✓ _____

3 **A:** _____ (your sister work) hard at the moment?
 B: ✗ _____

4 **A:** _____ (your brother study) French this year?
 B: ✓ _____

5 **A:** _____ (we work) in groups today?
 B: ✗ _____

6 **A:** _____ (I sit) in your place?
 B: ✗ _____

7 **A:** _____ (you wait) for your friends?
 B: ✓ _____

8 **A:** _____ (we win) at the moment?
 B: ✗ _____

9 **A:** _____ (Mr Davies watch) me?
 B: ✓ _____

Grammar Alive Describing a scene

7 *** **Look at the picture and complete the questions and answers.**

1 **A:** What / the / boys / do?
 What are the boys doing?
 B: *They are playing football.*

2 **A:** the girl / surf?
 _____
 B: _____

3 **A:** the man / climb?
 _____
 B: _____

4 **A:** What sport / the girls / play?
 _____
 B: They
 _____

5 **A:** What / the woman / do?
 _____
 B: She
 _____

6 **A:** the dog / swim?
 _____
 B: _____

Reading

1 Read the texts. Match the information below with the correct texts.

at a school   cycling or walking
going to school or work   in a shopping centre
playing sports and doing other activities   ~~walking~~

	What	Where
Text 1	1 *walking*	2 _____
Text 2	3 _____	4 _____
Text 3	5 _____	6 _____

1 Mall Walking started in the USA. Some people say shopping centres are the perfect place for some exercise for the over 60s or people who aren't fit enough to go to a gym and who think that the streets are too dangerous, and the weather too hot or too cold for walking.

Now you can join the first mall walking club of Great Britain. Get fit, look at the shops, meet some new friends and finish the day with a nice cup of tea.

£10 a year to join. Walks every Saturday afternoon
Phone: 08654372 or visit our website
www.mallwalkersuk.com

2

From:	Jeff
To:	Paul

No Car Day – 9 September
22 September is No Car Day, a day when people all over the world leave their cars at home and walk or cycle to work or school.

Help the planet and get fit at the same time. Leave your car at home on 22 September.

3

Sports Open Day
Leyton Park School is having a sports open day on Saturday 18 June

When:	2–5 p.m.
Where:	Leyton Park School, 12 Bush Lane, Leyton
Who:	All children aged 5–8 years old.
Activities:	running, jumping, sports, fun games and activities, parents' sports

Come and have fun. It's free.

2 Read the text again. Match the people (a-g) with the activities in the texts (1-3).

a Sam likes sports but he doesn't have any friends to do them with. He has a six-year-old son who loves games. _3_

b Helen has got two children aged six and seven who love sports. ___

c Natalie is seventy years old. She likes meeting people and wants to do some easy exercise. ___

d Mark works in a bank one kilometre from his home. He drives to work and never has time to do any exercise. ___

e Pat goes shopping every Saturday. She'd like to do some exercise as well but she doesn't have time to do both. ___

f Miranda has got a bike in her garage but she never uses it. She wants to start cycling more. ___

g Liam is in class 2C at a primary school. He loves running. ___

Sentence Builder *too/not enough*

3 Complete the sentences with the adjective in brackets, the correct form of the verb *be* and *too* or *not … enough*.

1 I don't want to play tennis. It *isn't exciting enough* (exciting) for me. Football is much better.

2 I want to run ten kilometres but I _____ (fit). I can't run one kilometre!

3 This game _____ (fast) for me. I can't see the ball.

4 I like surfing but I can't go to Hawaii to do it. I _____ (rich)!

5 I want to learn Russian but it _____ (difficult). French is easier.

6 I've got tennis rackets, footballs, skis and a skateboard in my room but I can't put my bike in there. My room _____ (big).

4 Match the adjectives (1-7) with their opposites (a-g).

1 big _____c_____   a cheap
2 hot _____   b young
3 fast _____   c small
4 expensive _____   d easy
5 difficult _____   e short
6 old _____   f slow
7 tall _____   g cold

5 Use the words in brackets to rewrite the second sentence.

1 We can't play football in my garden. It's too small. (enough)
We can't play football in my garden.
It _____isn't big enough._____

2 I can't climb up there. I'm not tall enough. (too)
I can't climb up there. I _____

3 I don't want to swim today. It isn't hot enough. (too)
I don't want to swim today. It _____

4 Everyone got 100 percent in the maths test. It was too easy. (enough)
Everyone got 100 percent in the maths test.
It _____

5 You can't do judo. You're not old enough. (too)
You can't do judo. You _____

6 We can't play games on this old computer. It's too slow. (enough)
We can't play games on this old computer.
It _____

Listening

6 ⟨27⟩ Listen to three conversations (1-3). Match them with the situations (a-d). There is one extra situation.

a A telephone conversation _____
b A meeting in the street _____
c A conversation at a party _____
d Someone coming to someone else's house _____

7 ⟨27⟩ Listen again. Are the sentences true (T) or false (F)?

1 Debbie is with her brother. _____F_____
2 Debbie goes to the sports day. _____
3 Jack's dad is at home. _____
4 Mr Davies wants to walk to work. _____
5 Amy is going to a party. _____
6 Derek agrees to meet Amy. _____

Word Builder Multi-part verbs (2)

8 Complete the phrases with the correct words. You can see the first letter of each word.

1 A: Hi, Hannah. What are you u_p_____ t_o_____ ?
B: I'm reading.

2 A: When can I see you?
B: C_____ r_____ here at seven o'clock.

3 A: Let's go dancing.
B: No, I'm n_____ i_____ the music they play at the disco.

4 A: It's too late to do anything now.
B: Oh, c_____ o_____ , Eliza. It's only nine o'clock.

5 A: Do you want to g_____ o_____ ?
B: No, I'm too tired.

9 Complete the dialogue with the complete phrases from Exercise 8.

Ian: Hello?
Neil: Hi, Ian. It's Neil. [1] _____What are you up to?_____
Ian: Hi, Ian. I'm watching the football on TV.
Neil: [2] _____ ?
Ian: No, it's a very good game.
Neil: [3] _____ , Ian. It's 0-0. It's boring. Let's go for a pizza.
Ian: No, [4] _____ pizza these days. I want to lose weight. And I want to watch the football.
Neil: Well, [5] _____ here after the football and play my new computer game with me.
Ian: Okay. See you in about half an hour.

15

Present Continuous: arrangements

1 * Complete the dialogue with the correct form of the verbs in brackets.

Jack: I'm bored.

Nick: Why don't you find something to do?

Jack: What can I do?

Nick: There are lots of things you can do. This is what I [1] *'m doing* (do) this weekend. On Friday evening, I [2]_____ (meet) Jane. We [3]_____ (go) to the cinema. Then on Saturday, Tom and I [4]_____ (play) tennis. Then we [5]_____ (have) lunch with Sam. After lunch, Tom and Sam [6]_____ (start) their new yoga classes. I [7]_____ (not go) with them because my dad [8]_____ (take) me to a basketball match.
It's my mum's birthday on Sunday. She [9]_____ (not have) a big party. We [10]_____ (have) lunch at a nice restaurant near our house.

Jack: Wow. You are busy. Can I come with you to the cinema on Friday?

Nick: Of course you can.

2 ** Use the cues to make questions about the dialogue.

1 Who / Nick / meet / on Friday?
Who is Nick meeting on Friday?

2 Where / they / go?
_____

3 What sport / Nick and Tom / play?
_____

4 When / they / play?
_____

5 Who / they / meet / for lunch?
_____

6 Nick / do / yoga with Tom and Sam?
_____

7 Where / his dad / take / him?
_____

8 Nick's mum / have / a big birthday party?
_____

9 Where / they / have / lunch?
_____

3 ** Complete the answers to the questions in Exercise 2 and match them with the correct questions.

1 He / meet / Jane
 He is meeting Jane.   1

2 He / take / him to a basketball match
_____

3 No, he / not
_____

4 They / go / to the cinema
_____

5 They / play / on Saturday morning
_____

6 They / have lunch / at a nice restaurant
_____

7 No, she / not
_____

8 They / meet / Sam
_____

9 They / play / tennis
_____

Grammar Alive Talking about arrangements

4 *** Use the cues to complete the dialogues.

1 **A:** you do / tonight?
 B: I / go / a disco
 A: *What are you doing tonight?*
 B: *I'm going to a disco.*

2 **A:** who / go / with?
 B: I / go / Laura and Beth
 A: _____
 B: _____

3 **A:** how / you / get there?
 B: we / go / bus
 A: _____
 B: _____

4 **A:** where / you / meet?
 B: we / meet / my house
 A: _____
 B: _____

5 **A:** you / come home / taxi?
 B: no / we / not. My dad / collect us at 11 p.m.
 A: _____
 B: _____

Speaking Workshop 5

❶ Complete the sentences with the words below.

give me   help me   ~~lend me~~   show me   tell me

1 Can you __*lend me*__ your mobile phone for a minute, please?

2 Can you _____ the answer to question two, please?

3 Can you _____ with this homework, please?

4 Can you _____ your photos, please?

5 Can you _____ my bag, please?

go   have   meet   play   watch

6 Could we _____ my computer game now?

7 Could we _____ lunch soon? I'm hungry.

8 Could we _____ to the theatre this weekend?

9 Could I _____ the film at eight o'clock, please?

10 Can we _____ at four o'clock, not three o'clock?

❷ Match the responses with the requests.

1 Can you help me to write this email, please?   _c_

2 Could we have a rest now?   ___

3 Can your dad take me to school with you?   ___

4 Could I borrow your pen, please?   ___

5 Can we listen to a different CD?   ___

6 Could you show me where we are on this map, please?   ___

a Yes, of course, come round at eight o'clock but don't be late because he hates waiting.

b No problem. Don't you like rap music?

c Of course. Who is it to?

d Sorry, I'm using it at the moment.

e I'm sorry, I can't. I don't know this area very well.

f Sure, no problem. I'm tired as well.

❸ 28 Complete the sentences with the correct words. You can see the first letter of each word. Then listen to check.

1 O*kay*_____ . Here we are.

2 That's okay. Okay, I_____ 's practise!

3 Sure. N_____ problem. Try this one.

4 I'm s_____ I can't because I'm playing tennis with Angela.

5 Okay. L_____'s stop now – I'm tired.

6 Fantastic!

7 Sorry, b_____ I need them. Your shoes are fine.

❹ 29 Complete the dialogue with Zoe's responses from Exercise 3 in the correct places. Then listen to check.

Patsy: Hey Zoe! I'm here!

Zoe: Patsy! I'm in the garden!

Patsy: Ooh! Look at you! Sorry, I haven't got any tennis clothes. Can you lend me a T-shirt, please?

Zoe: ¹*Sure. No problem. Try this one.*___

Patsy: Can you lend me a pair of trainers, please? I forgot to bring mine.

Zoe: ²_____

Patsy: All right. Back in a minute! ... How do I look?

Zoe: ³_____

Patsy: Can you lend me a racket, please?

Zoe: Okay. ⁴_____

Patsy: Oh ...

Zoe: And here's the tennis court!

Patsy: Computer tennis! Fantastic! Great idea! But, I'm not very good ...

Zoe: ⁵_____

Patsy: Yes! I'm enjoying this! It's better than normal tennis! Yes!

Zoe: ⁶_____

Patsy: Could we play again tomorrow?

Zoe: ⁷_____ .
Chocolate?

Patsy: Thanks! Tennis is great, isn't it? And I love chocolate!

Writing Workshop 3

1 **Read the notes and answer the questions.**

  1 Who is having a birthday party on Saturday?
     _____Ellen_____

  2 Who is making a cake? _____

  3 Who is organising the music? _____

  4 What is Rebecca's cousin's name? _____

  5 Who is having problems at university?
     _____

  6 Who can't come to the party? _____

---

¹   _____b_____

It's Ellen's birthday on Saturday ᵃ~~so~~/because we're
organising a party for her. She doesn't know about it.
Sue and Imelda are taking her for a pizza at six o'clock.
We're having the party at Imelda's house. Natalie's
making a cake and Dan is organising the music
ᵇso/because he's a great DJ!

²_____ Can you come at six to help us get the
room ready?

³ _____

⁴ _____

Hannah

Hi Hannah,

Thanks for the invitation. What a great idea!
⁵_____ . Can I bring my cousin, Tina?
She's sixteen and really friendly. ⁶_____
not at six o'clock ᶜso/because Tina is arriving at
7 o'clock.

See you on Saturday.

Cheers,

Rebecca

Hannah

Thanks for the invitation. ⁷_____
ᵈso/because we're going away for the
weekend. My brother is having problems at
university ᵉso/because we're going to try to
help him.

Thanks anyway. Have a great time!

Mel

---

2 **Read the messages again and complete them with
the phrases below in the correct gaps (1-7).**

  a I'd love to come.

  b Hi there

  c I can come but

  d Would you like to come?

  e See you.

  f I'm sorry but I can't come

  g Please send me a text or call me.

3 **Choose the correct words (a-e) in the notes.**

4 **Match the beginnings (1-6) with the correct
endings (a-f).**

  1 I can't come to the party because   _e_

  2 I've got a lot of homework to do so   ___

  3 My dad's taking me by car so   ___

  4 I don't know what time I can be there because ___

  5 I'm free all day on Saturday so   ___

  6 I'd love to come to your party because   ___

  a I can't come.

  b I can help you to organise the party.

  c I'm working on Saturday and I sometimes finish
late.

  d I love parties!

  e I'm going to a concert with Sam on Saturday
evening.

  f you can come with me.

5 **Look at the message from Adam. Write replies
from Jackie and Brian using the information below.**

Hi there,

I'm playing football on Saturday afternoon for the local
team. It's my first game so I'm a bit nervous. Would you
like to come and see me? Please come. I'd love to see
you all and have a pizza after the match.

Please send me a text or call me.

See you,

Adam

Jackie – can't – working all afternoon – love a pizza –
when and where?

Brian – can – not doing anything on Saturday – love
football – can't have pizza – meet Sandra at six o'clock

Sound Choice 3

Sound Check

Say the words and expressions below.

a lived, worked, wanted (Exercise 1)

b singing songs, thinking about, doing homework (Exercise 2)

c shower, share, dishwasher (Exercise 3)

d car, party, say, make (Exercise 4)

e laugh, late, bath, wait (Exercise 5)

f Can I borrow your phone, please? Could we leave soon? (Exercise 6)

g sixth, fifth, rugby (Exercise 7)

30 **Listen and check your answers. Which sounds and expressions did you have problems with? Choose three exercises to do below.**

1 **31** Grammar - Regular past endings **Write the words in the correct column depending on the sound of the final -ed. Then listen to check.**

live work want chat love ask download laugh show answer talk invite

/d/	/t/	/ɪd/
lived	worked	wanted

2 **32** Grammar - -ing endings **Listen and repeat the words and phrases.**

ing, singing, singing songs

ing, thinking, thinking about

ing, doing, doing homework

ing, working, working hard

ing, listening, listening to music

3 **33** Consonants **Listen to the words and say where the sh sound is. Write B (beginning of the word), M (middle of the word) or E (end of the word). Listen again and repeat the words.**

1 _B_ 2 ___ 3 ___ 4 ___ 5 ___
6 ___ 7 ___ 8 ___ 9 ___

4 **34** Vowels **Look at the words below. Which vowel sound do they have? Write them in the correct column. Then listen to check.**

~~party~~ make last table wake start

/a:/ car	/ei/ say
party	

5 **35** Spelling **Listen and write the words which are spelt with an ar and an ay. Don't write any of the other words.**

car	say
March	

6 **36** Expressions **Listen and repeat the expressions. <u>Underline</u> the word which is stressed in each sentence.**

1 Can I borrow your <u>phone</u>, please?

2 Could we leave soon?

3 Do you remember Mrs Smith?

4 And then you went home.

5 Sorry, I can't.

6 Sure, no problem.

7 **37** Difficult words **Listen and repeat eight words which have two or three consonant sounds together. Then write the words and <u>underline</u> the consonant clusters. Two words have two consonant clusters.**

1 _____sixth_____
2 _____
3 _____
4 _____
5 _____
6 _____
7 _____
8 _____

Check Your Progress 5

① **Activities** Complete the activities with the correct letters. Then complete the sentences with - or the correct form of *do* or *play*.

1 Tom likes _____ c_cl_n g.
2 Ellen _____ y_ g _ every day.
3 Mike often _____ ice h_c k _ _ .
4 Sam _____ j_d_ last year.
5 Mike loves _____ s_ r f _ _ g
6 Do you _____ a lot of _ x _ r c _ _ e?
7 We _____ a lot of _t h l _ t _ c _ at our school.
8 Can you _____ t_ b l _ t _ n n _ s?

/8

② **Present Continuous** Complete the sentences with the correct forms of the verbs below.

cook   drink   read   talk   walk   watch

What are the people in your family doing at the moment?
1 My dad _____ a film on TV.
2 My sister _____ a book.
3 My grandparents _____ dinner.
4 My mum _____ in the park.
5 My two brothers _____ to their friends on their mobile phones.
6 I _____ some water in the kitchen.

/6

③ **Present Continuous questions and answers** Use the cues to make questions and complete the answers.

1 **A:** What / you / read?
  _____
  B: _____ (I / read) an email from my friend.
2 **A:** Where / you / go now?
  _____
  B: _____ (I / go) to the tennis club.
3 **A:** Who / he / talk to on his mobile phone?
  _____
  B: _____ (He / talk) to his girlfriend.
4 **A:** _____ (I / wait) for my dad.
  B: What / he / do?
  _____
  A: _____ (He / buy) new skis.
  B: Why?
  A: _____ (He / go) on a skiing holiday next week.

/10

④ *Too/enough, so/because* **Complete the sentences with the correct words.**

1 I didn't buy the computer _____ it was _____ expensive.
2 We weren't quiet _____ in our exam _____ our teacher gave us extra homework.
3 We were _____ hot _____ we opened the window.
4 I didn't go to the night club _____ I wasn't old _____ to get in.
5 When we went cycling, we didn't wait for Simon _____ he was _____ slow.
6 My wardrobe isn't big _____ for all my clothes _____ a lot of them are on the floor.

/6

⑤ **Multi-part verbs (2)** Choose the correct words to complete the sentences.

1 'Do you want to ___ ?' 'Yes, okay. Where to?'
  a go out   **b** get in   **c** come round
2 'What are you ___ ?' 'I'm writing an email.'
  a into   **b** up to   **c** on to
3 'Do you like Kinect sports?' ' No, I'm not ___ computer games.'
  a up to   **b** on to   **c** into
4 'I don't really want to go to the concert.' 'Oh, ___ Steve. There are some great bands playing.'
  a come in   **b** come on   **c** come out
5 'When can I see you?' ' ___ to my house tomorrow afternoon.'
  a Get in   **b** Go out   **c** Come round

/5

TOTAL SCORE   **/35**

Module Diary 5

① **Look at the objectives on page 51 in the Students' Book. Choose three and evaluate your learning.**

1 Now I can _____ well / quite well / with problems.
2 Now I can _____ well / quite well / with problems.
3 Now I can _____ well / quite well / with problems.

② **Look at your results. What language areas in this module do you need to study more?**

6 AGE

TOPIC TALK - VOCABULARY

1 Complete the sentences with the words below.

about ~~baby~~ child fifty-one pensioner teenager months

1 Andy is a _____baby_____ . He's only six _____ old.
2 Aggie is a _____ . She's six years old.
3 Penny is fifteen years old. She's a _____ .
4 My mum is forty-five and my dad is _____ .
5 Ken is _____ seventy-five years old. He's a _____ .

2 Match the descriptions (1-9) with the correct jobs (a-i).

1 Lisa works with animals. She's a _d_
2 Steve works in a hospital. He's a ___
3 Amanda works in a school. She's a ___
4 Ellen works in an office. She's an office ___
5 Chris works on a bus. He's a bus ___
6 Sue works in a shop. She's a shop ___
7 My brother is at university. He's a university ___
8 Lenny works for the police. He's a police ___
9 My sister is in her first year at school. She's a ___

a assistant.
b student.
c driver.
d vet.
e primary school student.
f nurse.
g worker.
h officer.
i teacher.

3 Complete the adjectives with the correct letters.

1 Tia always puts things in their right place. Her desk is never covered in papers and her clothes are always in her wardrobe. She's very t_i_ _d_ _y_ .
2 Chris knows a lot and does well at school. He's very c_ _ _v _ _ _ .
3 Fiona always says 'Hello' and is nice to people. She's very f_ _ _ _n _ _ _ _ .
4 Kinga always helps people and is good to them. She's very k_ _ _ _ .
5 Harry always does his homework and studies a lot. He's very h_ _ _ _ - w_ _ k_ _ _ _ .
6 Oliver loves meeting new people. He's very o_ _ _g _ _ _ _ _ .
7 Melanie is sometimes unfriendly and not very nice. She's m_ _ _d _ _ .
8 Steve finds it hard to talk to people he doesn't know well because he's very s_ _ _ .
9 Tara always has something to say to her friends. She never stops talking. She's very t _ _ _ k _ _ _ _ v _ .

4 Match the beginnings (1-5) with the correct endings (a-e).

1 Eric is a _b_
2 He's sixteen ___
3 He is interested ___
4 He's a secondary school ___
5 He is very ___

a student.
b teenager.
c friendly.
d years old.
e in sport.

1 She was a ___
2 She is interested ___
3 Erica is a ___
4 She is about ___
5 She is very ___

a kind.
b seventy-five years old.
c vet.
d pensioner.
e in gardening.

Present Simple and Continuous

1 * Match the questions with the correct answers.

1 What do you do?   _a_
2 What are you doing?   _b_
3 What films do you watch? ___
4 What film are you watching? ___
5 Are you working?   ___
6 Do you work?   ___
7 What languages does he speak? ___
8 What language is he speaking? ___
9 Are class 5C doing a test? ___
10 Do class 5C do tests?   ___

a I'm a teacher.
b I'm cooking.
c It's called *Inception*. It's great.
d Horror films, action films … I like a lot of different films.
e Yes, I do. I work in a shop on Saturdays.
f Not at the moment. I'm relaxing.
g French, German and Russian.
h I think it's Italian.
i Yes, every Friday.
j Yes, sshhhh!

2 * Choose the correct verb forms to complete the sentences.

1 My grandfather always *sleeps/is sleeping* in the afternoon.
2 I usually *go/am going* to bed at ten o'clock.
3 We *do/are doing* a project at school this week.
4 Dan can't go out. He *works/is working*.
5 We often *have/are having* tests at school.
6 My dad *doesn't work/isn't working* on Saturdays.
7 I *read/am reading* a great book at the moment.
8 Mickey isn't here. I think he *plays/is playing* football.
9 My brother *watches/is watching* a lot of TV.
10 Wait a minute. I *talk/am talking* on the phone.

3 ** Complete the sentences with the correct form of the verb in brackets.

1 Ed can't hear you. He _is listening_ (listen) to his new CD.
2 I _____ (often feel) tired in the evening.
3 My brother _____ (never go) to sleep before eleven o'clock.
4 My mum _____ (not work) this week. She's on holiday.
5 My mum always _____ (wake up) first in our family.
6 My parents _____ (shop). They _____ (buy) some food for dinner.
7 I usually go to school by bus but I _____ (cycle) this week because I want to do some exercise.
8 My dad _____ (not often have) a shower in the morning.
9 The people in my street _____ (often play) loud music at night.
10 Sam _____ (not do) very well at school at the moment.

4 ** Complete the sentences with the correct form of the verb in capitals.

WATCH
Chris [1] _is watching_ a football match on the TV at the moment. He always [2]_____ football on Saturday afternoons.

DO
I usually [3]_____ my homework in my bedroom but today I [4]_____ it in the living room.

EAT
We [5]_____ pizza today. We [6]_____ (not usually) pizza but it's my brother's birthday and he loves pizza.

GO
My mum [7]_____ (not often) to bed before eleven o'clock but, this evening, she [8]_____ to bed at nine o'clock because she [9]_____ to New York tomorrow for a business meeting.

READ
My brother [10]_____ (not usually) books but he [11]_____ *Great Expectations* by Charles Dickens at the moment. He's got an exam on it soon.

USE
A: Can I use your computer?
B: No, sorry. My mum [12]_____ it. She [13]_____ (not often) use the computer but she needs it for her work.

5 *** **Complete the questions and answers.**

1 A: ¹What time / you usually / go to bed?

What time do you usually go to bed?

B: I ²_____ (usually go) to bed at ten o'clock but I ³_____ (not go) to sleep then. I ⁴_____ (read) until about half past ten. I ⁵_____ (read) a really good book at the moment.

2 A: ⁶When / your father / usually / get up?

_____

B: He ⁷_____ (usually get up) at seven o'clock on work days but this week ⁸_____ (he / get) up at six o'clock every morning because ⁹_____ (he / work) in London for the week. He ¹⁰_____ (not usually work) there but they ¹¹_____ (have) some important meetings this week.

3 A: ¹²your parents / sleep / at the moment?

_____

B: Yes, they are. They went to a party last night and they got home at 5 a.m. They ¹³_____ (not often go) out but, when they do, they have a good time.

A: ¹⁴So / what / you / do now? ¹⁵you / make / breakfast for them?

_____

B: No, ¹⁶_____ (I / cook) dinner. They ¹⁷_____ (not eat) breakfast when they're tired. They just drink coffee. A lot of coffee.

Grammar Alive Talking about activities

6 *** **Read the information and complete the dialogues.**

1 It is Saturday afternoon. Louisa is working in Beth's Café. Her friend, Mel, walks in …

Mel: Hello, Beth. What / you / do?

Beth: I / work

Mel: you / always / work on Saturdays?

Beth: Yes / . usually work/ from 9 a.m.–1 p.m. Today / work / until 6 p.m. because two waitresses aren't at work.

Mel: *Hello, Beth. What are you doing?*

Beth: *I'm working.*

Mel: *Do you always work on Saturday afternoons?*

Beth: *Yes, I do. I usually work from 9 a.m. to 1 p.m. Today I'm working until 6 p.m. because two waitresses aren't at work.*

2 It is Friday afternoon. Luke is at home when his friend Brad phones him …

Brad: Hi, Luke. You / do / anything this evening?

Luke: ✓ /. I / work.

Brad: Have you got a job? Where / you / work?

Luke: No. I've got a lot of homework to do.

Brad: you always / get / a lot of homework?

Luke: No, we / not but our teacher / prepare us / for exams.

Brad: Hi, Luke. _____

Luke: _____

Brad: Have you got a job?

_____

Luke: No, I've got a lot of homework to do.

Brad: _____

Luke: _____

3 Karen comes to her boyfriend's house on a Friday evening. He is busy in the kitchen.

Karen: Hello, Toby. You / cook?

Toby: ✓. My mum / work late today so I / help her

Karen: What / you / make?

Toby: Bolognaise.

Karen: Wow! You / often / cook?

Toby: No / not. Can you help me?

Karen: Of course. I can help you eat it, too.

Karen: Hello, Toby. _____

Toby: _____

Karen: _____

Toby: Bolognaise.

Karen: Wow! _____

Toby: _____ Can you help me?

Karen: Of course. I can help you eat it, too.

❶ Read the text and find the information.

1 Voting age in Austria now: _____sixteen_____

2 Voting age in Austria before 2007: _____

3 % of American sixteen to seventeen-year-olds who work: _____

4 Number of states where sixteen-year-olds can drive: _____

5 % of twelve to seventeen-year-olds in the USA who are interested in politics: _____

Austria can do it, why can't we?

In 2007, Austria was the first European country to give the vote to sixteen-year-olds.

Some countries outside the EU, like Cuba and Brazil, also have the vote at sixteen. Before that, the voting age in Austria was eighteen, the same as in all the other EU nations. So why did they change it? There are a number of reasons. The number of older people in Austria is growing. They are interested in things which are important to them like the price of food, pensions and hospitals. They aren't very worried about education or jobs for young people. Austria needs more young people to vote because their problems are different to old people's problems. Young people are interested in politics and want older people to listen to them and understand their problems. Not everyone agrees with the idea. Some young people don't and a lot of older people are against it but it works and it's a great idea.

So, why can't American sixteen to seventeen-year-olds vote? 80 percent of us work and pay money to the government. We can drive at sixteen in forty-eight of the fifty states. We are responsible enough to drive so we are responsible enough to vote. We are also interested in politics. The Washington Post found that 73 percent of all twelve to seventeen-year-olds are quite or very interested in politics and all of us learn about politics at school.

Join our campaign today!

TODAY | 23

❷ Read the text again. Choose the best answers to the questions.

1 Austria's voting age:
   a was always different to the voting age in other countries.
   b is now different to the voting age in all other countries.
   c is the same as some other countries in the EU.
   d is the same as some non-European countries.

2 Older people in Austria aren't very interested in:
   a education.
   b hospitals.
   c pensions.
   d food prices.

3 Which sentence about opinions on the new voting age in Austria is true?
   a Only young people agree with it.
   b All young people agree with it.
   c Some young people and some older people are against it.
   d All older people are against it.

4 Young people in the USA:
   a are all interested in politics.
   b all learn about politics at school.
   c are more interested in politics than older people.
   d can drive at sixteen in every state.

Word Builder Modifiers

③ Complete the sentences with *very*, *quite* or *not very* so they have the same meaning as the first sentence.

1 I love politics.
   I'm _____ *very* _____ interested in politics.

2 My room is small.
   My room is _____ big.

3 I don't often do my homework.
   I'm _____ hard-working.

4 My dad sometimes watches football on the TV but not always.
   My dad is _____ interested in football.

5 My mum is the best cook in the world!
   My mum is _____ good at cooking.

6 I usually get about 70 percent in my exams. I'm not the best in the class but I'm not the worst.
   I'm _____ clever.

7 Lisa never stops talking.
   Lisa is _____ talkative.

8 Pauline never smiles or says *Hello*.
   Pauline is _____ friendly.

Sentence Builder Information about people

④ Choose the correct words to complete the sentences.

1 **A:** Where are you *from*/*at*?
   B: I'm *from*/*at* Portsmouth.

2 **A:** What are you interested *on*/*in*?
   B: I'm interested *in*/*on* English and history.

3 **A:** What sports teams are you *on*/*in*?
   B: I'm *in*/*on* the football team.

4 **A:** What school are you a student *at*/*in*?
   B: I'm a student *at*/*in* Market Street School.

5 **A:** What year are you *on*/*in*?
   B: I'm *on*/*in* Year nine.

⑤ Look at the information about Corinne and complete the text.

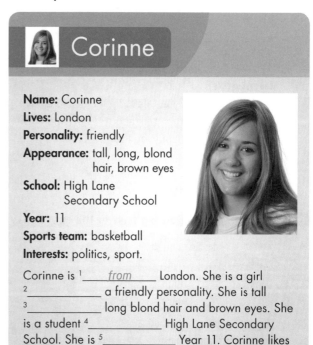

Corinne

Name: Corinne
Lives: London
Personality: friendly
Appearance: tall, long, blond hair, brown eyes
School: High Lane Secondary School
Year: 11
Sports team: basketball
Interests: politics, sport.

Corinne is [1] _____ *from* _____ London. She is a girl [2] _____ a friendly personality. She is tall [3] _____ long blond hair and brown eyes. She is a student [4] _____ High Lane Secondary School. She is [5] _____ Year 11. Corinne likes sport and is [6] _____ the girls' basketball team. She is interested [7] _____ sport and politics.

⑥ Look at the information about Matt and complete the sentences.

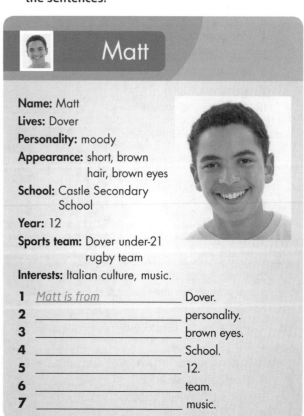

Matt

Name: Matt
Lives: Dover
Personality: moody
Appearance: short, brown hair, brown eyes
School: Castle Secondary School
Year: 12
Sports team: Dover under-21 rugby team
Interests: Italian culture, music.

1 *Matt is from* _____ Dover.
2 _____ personality.
3 _____ brown eyes.
4 _____ School.
5 _____ 12.
6 _____ team.
7 _____ music.

1 * Complete the questions with the correct words.

1 ___Where___ did you go last night? To Natalie's party.

2 _____ did you get there? At about eight o'clock.

3 _____ many people were there? About twenty-five.

4 _____ did you talk to? A girl called Emily.

5 _____ did you talk about? Films and music.

6 _____ time did you leave? At eleven o'clock.

7 _____ did you get home? By car.

8 _____ collected you? My dad.

2 * Read the information and answer the questions.

1 Sam loves Ann but she loves Ian. Ian doesn't love her. He loves Cathy but Cathy loves Sam.

1 Who loves Sam? ___Cathy___

2 Who does Sam love? _____

3 Who loves Ann? _____

4 Who does Ann love? _____

5 Who loves Ian? _____

6 Who does Ian love? _____

7 Who loves Cathy? _____

8 Who does Cathy love? _____

2 Paul, Nigel and Annie wanted to meet. Paul went to Nigel's house but he wasn't there. Nigel was at Annie's house but she was out. She was at Paul's house.

1 Who went to Nigel's house? _____

2 Where did Nigel go? _____

3 Who went to Annie's house? _____

4 Where did Annie go? _____

5 Who went to Paul's house? _____

6 Where did Paul go? _____

3 ** Look at the information and complete the questions.

Mandy wrote a letter to Barack Obama. His wife sent her a letter with a photo!

1 Who ___did Mandy___ write to? Barack Obama.

2 Who _____ to Mandy? Barack Obama's wife.

3 What _____ with the letter? A photo.

Will phoned his girlfriend, Lucy, last night to ask her to go the cinema. Her mother answered the phone. Lucy was out.

4 Who _____ phone last night? His girlfriend.

5 Why _____ her? To ask her to go to the cinema.

6 Who _____ the phone? Lucy's mum.

Grammar Alive Sharing personal information

4 *** Use the cues to make questions.

1 Where / you / live?
___Where do you live?___

2 How many people / live / in your home?
_____

3 What time / you start / school?
_____

4 Who / teach / you English?
_____

5 Which teacher / give / you the most homework?
_____

6 How much homework / you usually / get?
_____

7 Where / you go / last summer?
_____

8 Who / take / this photo of you?
_____

9 Where / you / buy / that CD?
_____

10 Who / give / you that T-shirt?
_____

Speaking Workshop 6

1 Label the pictures.

1 t*rousers*

2 s_____

3 d_____

4 c_____

5 s_____

6 j_____

7 j_____

8 h_____

Talk Builder Describing people in photos

2 Match the first sentences (1-5) with the sentences (a-e) which follow them.

1 This is a photo of my cousin.   _c_

2 I took lots of photos on holiday.   ___

3 I don't know which dress to buy.   ___

4 We had an exam in English.   ___

5 This is a photo of my two best friends.   ___

a What do you think? The red one or the blue one?

b It was a really difficult one.

c He's the one in the hat.

d The one on the left is Matt and the one on the right is Chris.

e This is the best one.

3 Complete the sentences with the correct words.

Megan: This is a photo of my family. That's me ¹_____*in*_____ the middle.

Isabel: Oh, yes. I like your hat! Who is that ²_____ your left?

Megan: That's my sister and that's my mum on my ³_____ .

Isabel: Is that your dad next ⁴_____ your mum?

Megan: No, that's my uncle. My mum's brother. You can't really see my dad. He's ⁵_____ the back. He isn't very tall but you can see his grey hair.

Isabel: So, these children sitting at the ⁶_____ - are they your cousins?

Megan: Three of them are my cousins but the ⁷_____ on the right is my little brother, Stuart.

Isabel: You've got a lovely family. Do you want to see a photo of my family?

4 〔38〕 **Use the cues to complete the dialogue. Then listen to check.**

1 **A:** This / photo / my family

2 **B:** Who / that / next / you?

3 **A:** That / cousin. name / Sandra

4 **B:** Where / your parents?

5 **A:** They / back and my brother / front

6 **B:** Which one / your brother

7 **A:** one / left. boy / next / him / his friend

   B: Have you got any more photos?

8 **A:** Yes / take / this / last summer …

1 **A:** *This is a photo of my family.*

2 **B:** _____

3 **A:** _____

4 **B:** _____

5 **A:** _____

6 **B:** _____

7 **A:** _____

   B: Have you got any more photos?

8 **A:** _____

Exam Choice 3

Reading

❶ Read the text and match the people (1-4) with the countries they are from (a-e). There is one extra country.

1 Jean Paul is seventeen and he wants to drive. He can't. ____

2 Claude is seventeen and he wants to get married. He can't. ____

3 Aina is nineteen and she can't vote yet. ____

4 Ed is seventeen and wants to leave school and get a job but he can't. ____

a Switzerland
b France
c Poland
d Great Britain
e Japan

What things are unfair in your country?

1 HOUR AGO

It's not fair!
Here in Japan, we can leave school and get a job when we are fifteen. We can get married and find somewhere to live when we are teenagers. We are not children. Now, we want to show how responsible we are by voting for our government. But we can't do that before we are twenty! Why not?

2 HOURS AGO

In Great Britain, young people can drive when they are seventeen. In the USA, they can drive when they are sixteen and in New Zealand, they can drive when they are fifteen! So why, here in France, can't I drive before my eighteenth birthday?

3 HOURS AGO

In many countries there are two ages at which people can get married. I understand why very young people need to ask their parents first. What I don't understand is that here in Switzerland, girls can get married when they are seventeen but boys have to wait until they are eighteen. Why is that?

5 HOURS AGO

When my grandfather was fourteen, he left school. My dad left school when he was sixteen. They wanted to work to help their families and so do I but I can't because now we can't leave school until we are eighteen. In the Czech Republic people can leave school when they are fifteen. Why isn't it the same here in Poland?

❷ Read the text again. Choose the best answer to the questions.

1 In Japan teenagers can't:
   a get married.
   b vote.
   c get a job.
   d leave school.

2 The earliest you can drive is in:
   a the USA.
   b Great Britain.
   c New Zealand.
   d France.

3 The writer doesn't understand why in Switzerland:
   a young people need to ask their parents before they get married.
   b girls and boys can't get married at the same age.
   c girls don't want to marry seventeen year old boys.
   d young people want to get married.

4 The school leaving age in Poland:
   a is two years later than it was when the writer's grandfather left school.
   b is the same as it was when the writer's father left school.
   c is three years later than in the Czech Republic.
   d was fourteen when the writer's father left school.

Listening

❸ 39 Listen to three dialogues(1-3) and match them with the situations (a-d). There is one extra situation.

Dialogue 1 ____
Dialogue 2 ____
Dialogue 3 ____

a At a party.
b At a sports lesson.
c At a shopping centre.
d In the street.

❹ 39 Listen again. Are the sentences true (T) or false (F)?

1 Rosy went to the same gym that Dana now goes to. ____

2 Rosy goes to the gym with Dana. ____

3 Lisa doesn't live in the same town as Frank. ____

4 It is Lisa's birthday party. ____

5 David came to the judo lesson because he saw information about the classes on TV. ____

6 Simon now has ten students in his class. ____

Speaking

5 Complete the dialogue with the words below. There are three extra words.

> could front left lend middle next one (x 2)
> problem sorry which

Roger: ¹_____ I look at your photos, please?

Adam: Sure, no ²_____ .

Roger: Who's that?

Adam: Where?

Roger: That boy. The ³_____ in the blue jumper.

Adam: Oh him. He's a friend of my brother's. That's my brother ⁴_____ to him.

Roger: What? On his ⁵_____ ?

Adam: Yes. And that's his girlfriend in the ⁶_____ of the photo. Her name's Sally.

Roger: She's nice. Can I see the next photo?

Adam: This is a good ⁷_____ . It's me and Harry on holiday.

Roger: Oh yes. I see Harry's at the ⁸_____ .

Adam: Yes, as always!

Use of English

6 Complete the text with the correct words. You can see the first letter of each word.

Dear Paul,

How are you? I'm having a great time here in Spain. The only problem is that my holiday isn't long ¹e _____ . At the moment, I'm sitting in my hotel room ²b _____ it's raining. So, I've got time to send you some photos. The first ³o _____ is of me swimming. The girl with me ⁴i _____ staying here. She's ⁵f _____ Ipswich. She's really nice ⁶w _____ a great personality. The second photo is of my favourite restaurant. The man next ⁷t _____ me is Carlos. He's a waiter at the restaurant. The girl ⁸o _____ the left works in the kitchen. She's a great cook. I love Spanish food!

See you soon,
Elaine

Choose the correct words to complete the sentences.

7 Choose the correct words to complete the sentences.

1 My father ___ at home at the moment. He's at work.
   a not **b** isn't **c** doesn't

2 Your problem is that you are ___ big enough to play rugby.
   a so **b** too **c** not

3 Could you ___ me your phone?
   a lend **b** use **c** borrow

4 I was tired ___ I went to bed early
   a but **b** because **c** so

5 Who ___ you with your homework?
   a helped **b** did help **c** did you help

6 My mum is ___ the left of the photo.
   a at **b** in **c** on

7 I want to buy a ticket but they are ___ expensive.
   a enough **b** too **c** more

8 I'm a student ___ Nottingham University.
   a at **b** in **c** on

Writing

8 Choose the correct words to complete the sentences.

1 Hi *here/there*.
2 Please *send/call* me.
3 *Send/Call* me an email.
4 Would you *like/want* to meet?
5 I'd love to come *and/but* I can't *so/because* I'm working all day.
6 I'm *sorry/sure* but I can't come.
7 *Cheers/Cheer*.

9 Write a message to some friends inviting them to a party.

- Say hello.
- Invite your friends to the party and give them details of when/where it is and what it is for.
- Ask them to contact you.

10 Write a reply to your friend.

- Thank your friend for the invitation.
- Tell your friend EITHER that you can come OR you can't.
- EITHER Give reasons why you can't come OR ask if you can bring a friend.

Check Your Progress 6

1 Occupations **Complete the sentences using the correct form of the words below.**

> assist   drive   engine   office   teach   wait

1 My uncle is a bus _____ . He drives the number 93.
2 I'd like to be an _____ but I need to learn about machines.
3 My mum is a _____ in a primary school. She likes children.
4 Jim's dad is a police _____ . He loves his job.
5 I work as a shop _____ on Saturdays in a big book shop.
6 Last summer, my sister worked as a _____ in a restaurant in Greece.

/6

2 Personality **Choose the correct words.**

1 Dan is very *shy/outgoing/tidy* and hates meeting new people.
2 Wow! Valerie does all her homework every night and then does more reading and writing. She's so *moody/hard-working/kind*.
3 Amy helped my grandmother with her shopping every day last week. She's so *talkative/kind/moody*.
4 My clothes are on the floor. My books are on the bed. I'm not very *tidy/shy/outgoing*!
5 I'm sorry I'm late. I met Rose and you know how *clever/outgoing/talkative* she is. She told me all about her family and her friends and her school.
6 Look. Johnny got 100 percent in his English, maths and French exams. He's so *tidy/clever/kind*.

/6

3 Present Simple and Continuous **Complete the sentences with the correct forms of the verbs in brackets.**

1 My brother _____ (not often eat) breakfast at home because he is always late for school. Today he _____ (eat) at home because it's Saturday.
2 (Sam watch) _____ TV at the moment? I know he usually _____ (watch) the basketball.
3 We _____ (not usually) start school at ten o'clock but we _____ (start) late this week.
4 'Where _____ (you go)?' 'To the cinema.' '_____ (you often go) to the cinema?'
5 Max _____ (not usually play) tennis well but he _____ (play) very well today.

/10

4 Subject and object questions **Complete the dialogue with a subject or object question.**

A: I got two emails today.
B: ¹_____ (Who / send) them?
A: Pauline and Heather.
B: ²_____ (What / they / say)?
A: Heather lives in France now.
B: Why ³_____ (she / live) in France?
A: Her dad works there.
B: Where ⁴_____ (Pauline / live)?
A: In Pagham. She's very excited. She's going to a party on Saturday.
B: Who ⁵_____ (invite) her?
A: A boy called Liam.
B: Where ⁶_____ (she / meet) him?
A: At her new school. She thinks you know him.
B: Who ⁷_____ (tell) her that?
A: Nikki. Liam plays tennis.
B: Oh! Liam Davies. Why ⁸_____ (Pauline / like) him?
A: I don't know. Why don't you write and ask her?

/8

5 Clothes **Complete the words with the correct letters.**

1 It's cold outside. Take your c__ __ __ .
2 Don't wear trousers. Wear a __ k __ __ t.
3 Magda is very beautiful in her long d__ __s__ .
4 She's wearing blue jeans and a grey t__ __ .
5 It's hot. Don't wear trousers. Wear s__o __ __s.

/5

TOTAL SCORE **/35**

Module Diary 6

1 **Look at the objectives on page 61 in the Students' Book. Choose three and evaluate your learning.**

1 Now I can _____ well / quite well / with problems.
2 Now I can _____ well / quite well / with problems.
3 Now I can _____ well / quite well / with problems.

2 **Look at your results. What language areas in this module do you need to study more?**

7 CINEMA

TOPIC TALK – VOCABULARY

1 **Put the words below in the correct columns.**

~~brilliant~~ dialogues actress funny animation
director science-fiction action scenes

Opinions	People	Types of film	Parts of a film
brilliant	_____	_____	_____
_____	_____	_____	_____

2 **Complete the types of films with the correct letters.**

1 *Toy Story, Finding Nemo* and *Cars* are all famous
a _n_ _i_ m _a_ _t_ _i_ _o_ n _s_ .
2 I don't like h _ _ _ _ _ films because I get scared.
3 I love films with exciting stories about love and history so I love d _ _ m _ _ .
4 *Notting Hill* is a r _ _ _ _ n _ _ _ c c _ _ _ _d_
with Hugh Grant and Julia Roberts.
5 Are the James Bond films the best a _ t _ _ _ _ films?
6 Harry Potter is the most popular f _ _ t _ _ _ _ film but *Lord of the Rings* is better.
7 *Speed* was a great t _ _ _ _ l_ _ _ _ starring Keanu Reeves and Sandra Bullock.
8 Clint Eastwood has been in a lot of w _ _ t _ _ n _ .
9 I watched an interesting d _c_ _ _ _ _ t _ _ _ _ film about the history of Hollywood.

3 **Match the beginnings (1-7) with the correct endings (a-g).**

1 It's a   *b*
2 The acting   ____
3 The special   ____
4 It's an exciting   ____
5 There are lots of great action   ____
6 The dialogues   ____
7 He's a great   ____

a are very funny.
b great film.
c director.
d story.
e is brilliant.
f scenes.
g effects are fantastic.

4 **Complete the text with the words below.**

acting action actor actress comedies ~~fiction~~
funny *Pirates of the Caribbean* scenes story

My favourite types of films are science-[1]___*fiction*___
films, thrillers and [2]_____ films. I don't like
romantic [3]_____ . I think they are boring.
My favourite [4]_____ is Matt Damon and my
favourite [5]_____ is Penelope Cruz.
My favourite film is [6]_____ - the first one
because it has got great action [7]_____ and it
is exciting and [8]_____ . The [9]_____
is easy to understand but clever - it's better than
in the other *Pirates of the Caribbean* films. I don't
understand them! The [10]_____ is brilliant -
especially Johnny Depp.

1 * Match the beginnings (1–8) with the endings (a–h).

1 Next year, I'm going to work _____d_____
2 My mum is going to look _____
3 My dad is going to buy _____
4 I'm not going to be _____
5 Suzie isn't going to play _____
6 My grandparents are going to move _____
7 Our teachers are going to give _____
8 I'm going to do _____

a late for school.
b exercise every day.
c us more tests.
d harder.
e tennis with Joanne again.
f for a new job.
g to a new house.
h a new car.

2 * Complete the sentences with the correct form of *be (not) going to* using the verb in brackets.

1 My friends and I ____are going to go____ (go) to the cinema every Friday next month.
2 I _____ (not spend) a lot of money when I go on holiday.
3 My sister _____ (not use) her mobile phone in class again.
4 My parents _____ (not eat) pizza every week because they want to lose weight.
5 We _____ (not stay) out late. See you at about nine o'clock.
6 I _____ (not chat) online to my friends until my exams finish.
7 My brother _____ (practise) the guitar everyday because he wants to be in a band.
8 I _____ (not watch) any more horror films! I didn't sleep at all last night.

3 ** Look at Mark's ideas. Make sentences using the correct form of *be (not) going to.*

Next year I'm going to change my life!

1 get up early ✓
2 watch a lot of television ✗
3 go swimming every morning ✓
4 be nervous before exams ✗
5 do my homework every day ✓
6 play computer games ✗
7 learn French ✓
8 do badly at school ✗
9 cycle on Saturdays ✓
10 go to school by car ✗

1 _Mark is going to get up early._____
2 _____
3 _____
4 _____
5 _____
6 _____
7 _____
8 _____
9 _____
10 _____

4 ** Here are some more of Mark's ideas. Complete them with the verbs below in the correct form.

be   buy   do   not forget   not go
learn   tidy   visit

1 _I'm going to be_ more friendly.
2 _____ shopping with my friends every week.
3 _____ yoga.
4 _____ my mum a nice Mothers' Day present.
5 _____ my girlfriend's birthday.
6 _____ my room every week.
7 _____ the local art gallery.
8 _____ how to cook.

5 *** Complete the questions and answers with the correct form of *be (not) going to.*

1 A: ¹What / you / do _What are you going to do_
for your project?
B: ²I / make / a film _____
A: What kind of film ³you / make? _____
B: I'm not sure but I know ⁴it / not / be
_____ a romantic comedy!

2 A: ⁵you / upload _____ your film to the
internet?
B: Yes, ⁶_____ . ⁷you / watch
_____ it?
A: Of course!

3 A: ⁸your brother / study _____ at film
school next year?
B: No, ⁹_____ ¹⁰He / study _____
English at university.

4 A: ¹¹your parents / buy _____ you a video
camera?
B: Yes, ¹²_____ Well, ¹³they / give
_____ me some money and ¹⁴I / buy it.
_____

5 A: Do you want to come round to my house on
Friday evening? ¹⁵We / watch a DVD.
_____
B: ¹⁶What film / you / watch? _____
A: I'm not sure. ¹⁷We / go _____ to the
DVD shop and get one.

Grammar Alive Talking about intentions

6 *** Use the cues to make dialogues.

1 A: I lose / my phone yesterday
B: What / going / do?
A: tell my parents
A: *I lost my phone yesterday.*
B: *What are you going to do?*
A: *I'm going to tell my parents.*

2 A: do badly / in my French exam last week
B: What / going / do
A: find a private teacher
A: _____
B: _____
A: _____

3 A: I see / a great video camera in the shopping
centre last Saturday
B: you / going / buy it?
A: Yes. I / get a Saturday job and save some
money
A: _____
B: _____
A: _____

4 A: Guess what I / do / tonight
B: you / watch a film?
A: No / not
B: you / do some work?
A: No / not
B: you / use the computer?
A: Yes / am
B: you / upload your photos?
A: Yes, / am. I / upload my holiday photos to my
website.
A: _____
B: _____
A: _____
B: _____
A: _____
B: _____
A: _____
B: _____
A: _____

1 🔘40 **Listen to someone answering questions about her job. Match her answers (dialogues a-e) with the topics below (1-6). There is one extra topic.**

1 What she does in the cinema.   ___
2 How many hours she works for.   _a_
3 How much money she gets for working there. ___
4 What she wears at work.   ___
5 What she likes about the job.   ___
6 The people she works with.   ___

2 🔘40 **Listen again and complete the information.**

HOURS OF WORK:	Friday: 6 p.m. – ¹ _11 p.m._
SATURDAY:	² _____ – 8 p.m.
UNIFORM:	Black trousers, black ³ _____, ⁴ _____ shirt
WHAT SHE GETS FREE:	Two free ⁵ _____ a week and ⁶ _____ at the end of her work
NUMBER OF PEOPLE WORKING AT THE CINEMA:	⁷ _____ She knows two of the girls from ⁸ _____

Sentence Builder *like* and *would like*

3 **Complete the sentences with *like* or *'d like*.**

1 I ____*like*____ going to the cinema but I ____*'d like*____ to stay at home tonight.
2 I _____ Italian food but I _____ to eat Chinese food tonight.
3 I _____ going on holiday but I _____ to work in a restaurant next summer.
4 I _____ to be an actor but I _____ being in a band, too.
5 I _____ having an older brother but I _____ to have a younger sister, too.

4 **Make questions for the answers.**

1 *Do you like watching films?*
   (like / watch / films?)
   Yes, I do. I love watching films.
2 _____
   (like / go to the cinema on Friday?)
   Yes, I would. That would be great. Thanks.
3 _____
   (like / read about actors and actresses?)
   No, I don't. I'm not interested in their private lives.
4 _____
   (like / meet / Johnny Depp?)
   Of course I would. That would be cool.
5 _____
   (like / go / to the cinema alone?)
   I don't mind. You can't talk when you're watching a film, can you?
6 _____
   (be / an actor?)
   No, I wouldn't. I'd like to be a singer.

Reading

5 Read the texts. Decide what the intention of the writer is.

1 talk about a festival that he/she went to ___
2 recommend the best festival to go to ___
3 describe the festivals and the films they show ___
4 warn people about problems they may face at the festivals ___

Cinemas are okay most of the year but, on a warm summer evening, it's great to watch a film outside. Here are some of the best outdoor festivals:

1 **Screen on the Green, Atlanta, Georgia**
Free movies in Atlanta's Piedmont Park. Up to ten thousand people watching each film, great films like *Back to the Future* and *Jurassic Park*. There were a few problems in 2010 but, don't worry, it's safe and great fun. It takes place in June and films start at about 9 p.m.

2 **The Guadalajara International Film Festival**
is a great place to see new Mexican films and independent films from many other countries. At the twenty-second festival, there were a total of 402 films and 66,000 people. The festival takes place in March when the weather is dry and warm. Guadalajara is a big city with some beautiful old buildings and great museums and art galleries.

3 **The Outdoor Cinema Food Fest**
takes place in San Francisco. On each day of the festival there is a film, a band, and there are food stalls which sell great food to the people at the festival. The festival takes place on Saturdays and lasts all summer from May to September. There are thrillers, comedies and science-fiction films and they are all very famous.

6 Read the text again. Match the people (a-d) with the best festivals for them (1-3). There is one extra person.

a Sally is learning Spanish and loves watching Spanish language films. She isn't interested in big Hollywood films. _2_

b Eleanor likes big Hollywood films. She's also into music. She goes to school from Monday to Friday but is free at the weekend. ___

c Nigel loves reading about celebrities and wants to go to a festival where he can see the stars and take their photographs. ___

d Ed loves films of all kinds. He works at weekends but can go to a festival from Monday to Friday. He loves being in a big group of people. ___

Word Builder -ed/-ing adjectives

7 Complete the dialogues with the correct form of the adjectives in brackets.

1 **A:** Was it a good film?
   B: No, it wasn't very _interesting_ (interest). In fact, it was really _____ (bore).

2 **A:** I'm always very _____ (tire) after a day at work. I can't do anything in the evening.
   B: Why don't you watch a film?
   A: I always fall asleep. Sometimes, I put on the most _____ (excite) film that I really want to see but I always fall asleep.

3 **A:** I'm an actor. Acting is a very _____ (tire) job. It isn't _____ (relax) at all. Are you _____ (relax)?
   B: No way. I'm a teacher!

8 Complete the sentences with the correct form of the adjectives below.

> bore (x 2)   excite   interest   relax   tire

1 I'm ___bored___ . I've got nothing to do.
2 Do you think yoga is _____ ? Oh yes. It's great. All my troubles go after an hour of yoga.
3 I'm _____ . I didn't sleep last night.
4 The film was _____ . Nothing happened.
5 Ben was very _____ about his birthday presents. He woke up at 5 a.m. and wanted to open them then.
6 This is a very _____ book about the history of the cinema. I'm learning a lot.

LESSON 21

GRAMMAR
have to/not have to

1 * Choose the correct words to complete the sentences.

I'm an actor
1 I *have to/don't have to* learn my words.
2 I *have to/don't have to* do homework.
3 I *have to/don't have to* listen to the director.
4 I *have to/don't have to* act.

Steve is a student.
5 He *has to/doesn't have to* do his homework.
6 He *has to/doesn't have to* go to school at the weekend. His lessons are from Monday to Friday.
7 He *has to/doesn't have to* teach the class.
8 He *has to/doesn't have to* listen to the teacher.

Dan and Julie are parents.
9 They *have to/don't have to* look after their children.
10 They *have to/don't have to* do what their children tell them.
11 They *have to/don't have to* watch TV every day.
12 They *have to/don't have to* buy food for their family.

2 ** Complete the sentences with the correct form of *(not) have to*.

We need young people to work as waiters and waitresses in a busy restaurant. 6 p.m.–11 p.m. Fridays and Saturdays.
1 You ___*have to*___ work hard.
2 You _____ cook the food.
3 You _____ be friendly and helpful.
4 You _____ get up early.
My brother is a university student. He has got a lot of work to do. He's got a room in a student house. No parents, no adults!
5 He _____ tidy his room.
6 He _____ go to the library to read books.
7 He _____ come home early. He can stay out all night if he wants to.
8 He _____ pass his exams in June.
My grandfather is a pensioner.
9 He _____ go to work.
10 He _____ take my grandmother to the doctors.
11 He _____ rest in the afternoon because he gets tired.
12 He _____ get up early but he likes getting up at seven o'clock.

3 ** Complete the text with the phrases below. There are two extra phrases.

don't have to get up   doesn't have to take   has to help
has to take   has to work   have to do   have to get up
have to go   have to make   have to take   have to tell
~~have to tidy~~   have to wash

A: What do you have to do at home?
B: I [1] ___*have to tidy*___ my room every Saturday. I [2] _____ my homework and I [3] _____ to bed at eleven o'clock. From Monday to Friday, I [4] _____ at seven o'clock but at the weekend, I [5] _____ early. I can stay in bed.
My brother [6] _____ my mum in the kitchen and I [7] _____ the car every Sunday. We [8] _____ breakfast in the morning and my brother [9] _____ the dog for a walk.
We can go out on Friday and Saturday evenings but we [10] _____ our mobile phones and we [11] _____ our parents what time we are coming home.

Grammar Alive Talking about obligations

4 *** Complete the dialogues with the correct form of *have to*.

1 **A:** you / go to bed early on Saturdays?
   B: ✗ but / go to bed early / from Sunday to Thursday
   A: *Do you have to go to bed early on Saturdays.*
   B: *No I don't but I have to go to bed early from Sunday to Thursday.*

2 **A:** you / help your parents in the kitchen?
   B: ✓ and / do the shopping on Saturdays
   A: _____
   B: _____

3 **A:** you / tidy your room?
   B: ✓ and / clean the living room
   A: _____
   B: _____

4 **A:** you / wear a uniform at school?
   B: ✗ but we / wear a white shirt
   A: _____
   B: _____

5 **A:** you / play rugby at school?
   B: ✗ but we / do gymnastics
   A: _____
   B: _____

Speaking Workshop 7

1 Complete the sentences with the words below.

agree   her   him   ~~it~~   neither   them   too   true

1 A: That was a great film.
   B: I didn't like _____it_____ .
   A: I love the James Bond films.
   B: Really? I don't like _____ .
2 A: I always eat popcorn when I go to the cinema.
   B: Me _____ .
3 A: Fantasy films are boring.
   B: I don't _____ .
4 A: Julia Roberts is coming to our local theatre.
   B: I don't like _____ .
5 A: Ben Stiller is a very funny actor.
   B: That's _____ .
6 A: Jason Statham is in this film.
   B: I don't like _____ .
7 A: I don't like 3D films.
   B: Me _____ .

2 Choose the best reply.

1 Oh great! Popcorn!
   ⓐ I don't like it.
   b I don't like him.
   c I don't agree.
2 I'm never going to watch another romantic comedy.
   a That's true.
   b Me too.
   c Me neither.
3 The special effects in this film aren't very good.
   a Me too.
   b Me neither.
   c That's true.
4 Some old black and white films are really good.
   a I don't like them.
   b Me too.
   c I don't like it.
5 Russell Crowe isn't very good in *Robin Hood*.
   a I don't agree.
   b I don't like it.
   c Me neither.
6 I think cinema tickets are too expensive.
   a Me neither.
   b Me too.
   c I don't like them.

3 Complete the dialogues with the correct words.

1 A: I love old films.
   B: Me _____too_____ .
2 A: This is a great film.
   B: I don't like _____ .
3 A: Emma Watson is great in this film.
   B: That's _____ .
4 A: I didn't like the fifth Harry Potter film.
   B: Me _____ .
5 A: *The Matrix* is the best film ever.
   B: I don't _____ .

4 🔊 41 Complete the dialogue with the phrases below. Then listen to check.

a I don't like his new film.
   Me neither.
b He's a brilliant actor.
   That's true.
c I love watching those old films.
   Me too.
d And that new pirate film was really boring.
   I don't agree.
e It's a brilliant film.
   I don't like it.

Gary: Hey, Patsy. Look there's a new film club this Saturday.
Patsy: Mm, that's really interesting.
Gary: Yeah.
Patsy: [1]*I love watching those old films.*
Gary: _____Me too._____ What have they got?
Patsy: *Casablanca*!!! It's my number one favourite. It's so romantic! [2]_____
Gary: _____ It isn't in 3D so I'm not interested! But real old classics like *Back to the Future*, or *Gremlins*, I love them!
Patsy: Those are all special effects! I prefer films with great actors, like Johnny Depp! [3]_____
Patsy: _____ He's in some really good films. But [4]_____
Gary: _____
Patsy: [5]_____
Gary: _____ I love all the *Pirates of the Caribbean* films. And Depp is fantastic.

Writing Workshop 4

1 Read the information about a film competition. Complete the email with the phrases below.

> ### Romford Film Festival - competition!
> We are holding an outdoor film festival on 3rd and 4th July. You can win free tickets in our great competition. Just write an idea for a new film! It has to be your own idea. The best five ideas will win FREE tickets to the festival and there will be a special prize for the best idea. For more information, please email us at romfordfilmfest@essex.com

closing date   Do I have to   How long   I am writing
I look forward   I would also   I would like
~~Sir/Madam~~   Yours faithfully,

From:	Charlie
To:	Info

Dear ¹ _Sir/Madam_ ,
² _____ to ask for information about your film competition. I am very interested in films. I enjoy writing too and would be interested in entering the competition.
³ _____ more information about the competition. ⁴ _____ does the writing have to be? What is the ⁵ _____ to send our ideas?
⁶ _____ like to ask about the prizes.
⁷ _____ go to the festival myself? I'm fourteen years old and I don't live near Romford so I can't go to the festival but I know other people who I could give the tickets to. Could I do that?
⁸ _____ to hearing from you.
⁹ _____

Charlie Stanford

2 Look at two different ways to write sentences. Use the words in brackets to rewrite the second sentences.

I enjoy writing, too.   I also enjoy writing.

I would also like to ask about the prizes.
I would like to ask about the prizes, too.

1 I enjoy writing. I'm also interested in films. (too)
I enjoy writing. I'm _____interested in films, too_____ .

2 I'd like to know the closing date, too. (also)
I'd _____ .

3 I like thrillers and I like comedies, too. (also)
I _____ .

4 You can meet actors and you can also win great prizes. (too)
You _____ .

3 Use the cues to make questions and sentences to use in an email to the cinema.

> ### NEW CINEMA OPENING ON 15 MARCH
> We have 100 free tickets to give away in a great, fun competition.
> **Win a ticket today!**
> Email us for more information at newodeon@offer.com

1 I / write / information / your competition
I am writing to ask for information about your competition.

2 enjoy / go / cinema and / love / chance / win a free ticket
_____

3 like / ask / the competition
_____

4 What / I / have / do / win ticket?
_____

5 When / closing date / for competition?
_____

6 also / information / the tickets
_____

7 Which films / tickets / for?
_____

8 I / only fourteen / can't go / all films
_____

9 also / only go / Fridays / at the weekend
_____

10 forward / hear / you
_____

4 Write an email to the cinema asking for more information about the competition. Use the ideas in Exercise 3.

- Start the email formally.
- Explain why you are writing and give some personal information.
- Ask questions about the competition and closing date.
- Ask questions about the prizes and explain why you want to know.
- End the letter formally.

80

Sound Choice 4

1 **43** Grammar - Contractions **Listen to the phrases and write the words which are contractions.**

1 _____aren't_____
2 _____
3 _____
4 _____
5 _____
6 _____

2 **44** Grammar - Unstressed *to* **Repeat the sentences.**

1 I have to tidy my room.
2 I'm going to work harder.
3 We're going to have a party.
4 She has to do her homework now.
5 They have to go home.
6 He's going to phone later.

3a **45** Consonants **Listen to the words and write *1* next to the word which the speaker says first.**

1 wash	_1_	watch	___
2 share	___	chair	___
3 ship	___	chip	___
4 sheep	___	cheap	___

3b **46** **Listen to more words with the sound /tʃ/ and repeat them.**

children, chat, picture, church, furniture, March, watch, much

4 **47** Vowels **Listen to the sentences. Write the word in each sentence with the same vowel sound as the ones in the box.**

/uː/ **food**	/ʌ/ **run**
too	_____
_____	_____
_____	_____

5 **48** Spelling **Listen and <u>underline</u> the silent letters in each word.**

1 cupboard
2 twelfth
3 talkative
4 dialogues
5 scenes
6 write

6 **49** Expressions **Listen and repeat the expressions.**

1 That's true.
2 Me too.
3 I'm on the right.
4 Me neither.
5 Who's that in the front?
6 I don't agree.

7 **50** Difficult words **Listen and repeat the schwa /ə/ sound. Then listen and repeat the words and write the word with a different *er* sound in the space below.**

worker, dancer, teacher, engineer, pensioner, teenager, driver, waiter

_____

Check Your Progress 7

1 Film **Complete the words with the correct letters.**

I went to the cinema last week. The film was a
[1]r _ m _ _ t _ _ c _ _ _ _ d _ . It was okay but the
[2]d _ _ l _ _ u _ _ weren't very funny. The
[3]a _ _ _ n _ wasn't very good. The main
[4]a _ _ o _ is usually funny but this wasn't his
best film. The [5]a _ _ r _ _ _ _ he was 'in love
with' wasn't right for him. I don't know why the
[6]d _ _ _ c _ _ _ decided to give her the part.
There was some nice [7]p _ _ t _ _ r _ _ _ y.
They were on holiday in Venice. There weren't any
[8]s _ _ c _ _ l e _ _ _ _ c _ _ but next week I'm
going to see a [9]s _ _ _ n _ _ -f _ _ t _ _ _ film.
It's going to be much better.

/9

2 *Going to* **Look at the plans. Complete the questions and answers.**

> **Plans for Saturday:**
> Me – go shopping
> **Plans for Sunday**
> Jo and Kate – watch a film
> Sam – play football
> My mum and dad – relax in the garden
> Me – listen to my new CD
>
> *What are you going to do on Saturday?*
> *I'm going to go shopping.*

1 A: What _____ Sunday?
2 B: They _____ a film.
3 A: What _____ Sunday?
4 B: He _____ football.
5 A: What _____ Sunday?
6 B: They _____ the garden.
7 A: What _____ Sunday?
8 B: I _____ CD.

/8

3 *-ed/-ing* adjectives **Complete the sentences with the correct form of the adjectives in brackets.**

1 It's a _____ book and I'm _____
every time I start reading it. (bore)
2 I was very _____ in the lesson because our
teacher is very _____ in history. (interest)
3 We were all very _____ about the school
trip but it wasn't an _____ trip at all. (excite)
4 Studying for exams is very _____ . I get
_____ when I open my school books. (tire)
5 My friend is a very _____ sort of person
but he hates doing _____ activities. (relax)

/5

4 *(not) have to* **Use the cues to make questions and answers.**

1 What time / Jo / have / get up in the morning?
2 He / have / get up at six o'clock.

_____
_____

3 / you / have / wear a uniform at school?
4 Yes, we / . We / have / wear a jacket and trousers.

_____
_____

5 / your mum / have / work on Saturdays?
6 No, she / not but / have / work on Mondays.

_____
_____

7 How much homework / you / have / do every day?
8 We / have / do one hour of homework every day.

_____
_____

/8

5 Agreeing and disagreeing **Complete the dialogue. There are three extra words.**

agree   also   like   me   neither   think   too   true

A: I don't understand this film.
B: Me [1]_____ . The acting is very poor.
A: Oh, I don't [2]_____ . I think the actors are
okay. It's the story that I don't like – it's too long.
B: That's [3]_____ . I think two hours is long
enough for a film.
A: Me [4]_____ . Let's watch *Transformers*.
B: I saw that at the cinema. I didn't [5]_____ it.

/5

TOTAL SCORE   **/35**

Module Diary 7

1 **Look at the objectives on page 71 in the Students' Book. Choose three and evaluate your learning.**

1 Now I can _____ well / quite well /
with problems.
2 Now I can _____ well / quite well /
with problems.
3 Now I can _____ well / quite well /
with problems.

2 **Look at your results. What language areas in this module do you need to study more?**

TOPIC TALK - VOCABULARY

1 Put the words into the correct part of the table.

beef broccoli cheese crisps kiwi lamb melon onion pasta rice salmon sardines sweets yoghurt

Meat	_beef_
Fruit	
Vegetables	
Cereals	
Fish	
Dairy	
Snacks	

2 Choose the word that is a different kind of food to the others.

1 apple	banana	lemon	(pork)
2 beans	eggs	lettuce	mushrooms
3 bread	milk	pasta	rice
4 beef	carrot	lamb	pork
5 nuts	salmon	sardines	tuna
6 cereal	cheese	egg	yoghurt
7 coffee	fruit juice	tea	tomato
8 cakes	chocolate	nuts	salmon

3 Complete the foods.

1 It's a fish. t_una_
2 It's meat from a pig. p_____
3 It's a dairy product from a hen. e_____
4 It's an orange vegetable. c_____
5 It's a snack made from two pieces of bread with something inside them. s_____
6 It's a drink made from things like oranges or apples. f_____ j_____
7 It's a hot drink you can have with milk or with lemon. t_____

4 Complete the words with the correct letters.

What I eat
For breakfast, I have ¹c _e_ _r_ _e_ _a_ _l_ with ²m __ __ k and I drink ³o __ __ n __ e j __ __ __ __ e. I never drink ⁴c __ __ __ ee but I sometimes drink ⁵t __ a. I eat lunch at school. I have fruit – a ⁶b__ __ __ __ __a or an ⁷a __ __ __ e. I also have ⁸c __ __ __ __ __ t __ and bread with ⁹ch__ __ __e. A lot of my friends eat snacks like ¹⁰c__ __ s __ s or ¹¹b __ __ c __ __ __ s but I don't. For dinner, we always have ¹²m__ __t and ¹³v __ __ __ t __ __ __ __ s. We don't often have ¹⁴b __ __ f or ¹⁵l __ __ b. We usually have ¹⁶c__ __c__ __n or ¹⁷f __ __ h with ¹⁸r __ __ e or ¹⁹p __ __ __ t __ __s and ²⁰b__ __c __ __ __ i or ²¹b__ __n__ .

5 Choose the correct words to complete the sentences.

1 I usually eat a lot of _a_ and vegetables.
   a fruit   b beans   c onions
2 I don't eat a lot of ___ food.
   a meat   b fruit   c dairy
3 I drink a lot of ___ .
   a melons   b water   c strawberries
4 I don't drink ___ .
   a cakes   b cola   c cabbages
5 My favourite meal is ___ .
   a dinner   b cereal   c meat
6 I often eat ___ like nuts or popcorn.
   a cereals   b snacks   c meals

① * Complete the predictions with *will* or *won't*.

In 2050 …

1 people ___won't___ cook. (✗)
2 people _____ grow vegetables in their homes. (✓)
3 restaurants _____ sell healthy fast food. (✓)
4 people _____ eat meat. (✗)
5 farmers _____ have animals. (✗)
6 food _____ be easy to grow. (✓)
7 food _____ be cheap. (✓)
8 people _____ take a lot of vitamins. (✓)
9 English food _____ be more popular than Italian food. (✗)
10 people _____ buy dinner from machines. (✓)

② * Complete the dialogue with the correct form of the verb in brackets.

Natalie: Do you want to go on holiday to France with me?
Sandra: I don't know.
Natalie: Come on. ¹___We'll have___ (We / have) a great time. ²_____ (We / eat) good food, ³_____ (we / meet) a lot of nice people, ⁴_____ (your French / get) better and ⁵_____ (we / not spend) a lot of money.
Sandra: Well …
Natalie: ⁶_____ (It / not rain), ⁷_____ (we / go) to Paris and ⁸_____ (we / buy) some cool clothes.
Sandra: ⁹_____ (I / not see) Jack for two weeks. ¹⁰_____ (He / find) another girlfriend.
Natalie: ¹¹_____ (No / not) ¹²_____ (He / be) there when you get back. He loves you!

③ ** Complete the sentences with future time expressions. The second sentence has the same meaning as the first.

It is Monday.
1 Will you cook dinner for me on Tuesday?
Will you cook dinner for me t___omorrow_____ ?

It is January 1ˢᵗ.
2 Will it snow on 15 January? I hope so, I'm going skiing.
Will it snow i_____ t_____ w_____ t_____ ? I hope so, I'm going skiing.
3 We're having an exam on Monday 8 January. It'll be difficult.
We're having an exam n_____ w_____ . It'll be difficult.

It is 2020.
4 Will you still love me in 2030?
Will you still love me i_____ t_____ y_____ t_____ ?

It is January.
5 I'll stop eating fast food in February.
I'll stop eating fast food n_____ m_____ .
6 I think I'll go on a cookery course in July.
I think I'll go on a cookery course i_____ s_____ m_____ t_____ .

④ *** Complete the questions and answers.

1 **A:** ¹_____What will you do_____ (What / you / do) when you leave school?
B: I don't know. I think ²_____ (I / go) to university or ³_____ (I / find) a job … or ⁴_____ (I / marry) a rich man!

2 **A:** ⁵_____ (you / go / travelling) next year?
B: I'd love to. The questions is: ⁶_____ (I / have) any money?
A: You're going to work this summer. ⁷_____ (you / have) some money from that.
B: ⁸(No, / not) _____ . There are a lot of things I want to buy.

3 **A:** ⁹_____ (you / stay) in this town in the future?
B: No way!
A: ¹⁰_____ (Where / you live)?
B: In an exciting city like London or New York. ¹¹_____ (I / not have) enough money to buy a house. ¹²_____ (I / get) a room in a house with some other young people. ¹³_____ (we / have) parties every night. ¹⁴_____ (it / be) great!

5 *** **Look at the information. Make questions and short answers.**

I'm going to Italy next month.

1 eat pizza? ✓
Will you eat pizza?
Yes, I will.

2 drink wine? ✗
_____
_____

3 the food be good? ✓
_____
_____

4 it be warm? ✓
_____
_____

5 it rain? ✗
_____
_____

6 the people be friendly? ✓
_____
_____

7 your parents be relaxed? ✗
_____
_____

8 people understand your Italian? ✓
_____
_____

6 *** **Complete the dialogue with the phrases below. There are three extra phrases.**

> it will   it will be   I will start   they'll be
> they'll give (x 2)   they will   will I start   will it be
> will they give   will you get   you'll get   you'll like
> you won't finish

A: I don't know what to do this summer.
B: Get a job.
A: Where?
B: At the restaurant in King Street. They always need people. [1] *They'll give* you work.
A: [2]_____ difficult?
B: Yes, [3]_____ . It's always busy there. But [4]_____ a lot of money.
A: What time [5]_____ in the mornings?
B: About eleven o'clock but [6]_____ before 11 p.m.
A: [7]_____ me a break?
B: Yes, [8]_____ , and [9]_____ you food.
A: Hmm, I'm not sure.
B: [10]_____ it. They're really friendly. Tell them that I told you to go there. [11]_____ very happy. They like me.

Grammar Alive Predicting the future

7 *** **Make dialogues between the man and the fortune-teller.**

1 A: rich?
B: ✓ but / give all money to poor people
A: *Will I be rich?*
B: *Yes, you will but you will give all your money to poor people.*

2 A: learn a new language?
B: ✓ – learn / German, Russian and Chinese
A: _____
B: _____

3 A: be famous?
B: ✗ but fifty-two people / read your blog
A: _____
B: _____

4 A: have a lot of children?
B: ✓ – have / three girls and two boys
A: _____
B: _____

5 A: find an interesting job?
B: ✓ – be / an English teacher
A: _____
B: _____

6 A: have a nice car?
B: ✗ but have / great bike
A: _____
B: _____

7 A: pass all my exams?
B: ✗ but / pass them next year
A: _____
B: _____

8 A: learn how to cook?
B: ✗ but / marry a good cook
A: _____
B: _____

1 Read the text. Match the <u>underlined</u> words with the correct meanings (a–f).

1 very good ___*amazing*___

2 something or someone that a lot of people know about _____

3 activities which explain and show how to do something or how something works _____

4 people working or helping because they want to, not for money _____

5 the animals that the meat beef comes from _____

6 offer to do something for no money _____

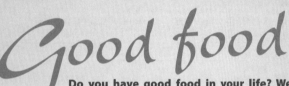

Good food

Do you have good food in your life? We asked for some ways that you get good food. Here are a few of your stories.

Our school has got an organic garden. We learn about growing vegetables and looking after them in our food science lessons. In the holidays, we can <u>volunteer</u> to work in the garden. My family live in a flat so it's great for me to have a garden at school. <u>Volunteers</u> can take some vegetables home too, so my parents are very happy that I like working there.

My aunt and uncle live on a farm in Wales. It isn't very big but they've got hens, pigs and <u>cows</u>. We always go to stay with them in the summer. It's a beautiful place and the food is <u>amazing</u>. All the vegetables are so fresh and, because the farm is organic, we know they are healthy, too.

We live in Lincoln and my parents buy food at The Pink Pig Farm Shop. It's very <u>famous</u> in Lincolnshire and all the food they sell is from animals that live on the farm or vegetables that they grow. They organise a food festival once a year and we always go to eat the free food and watch cookery <u>demonstrations</u>. They are really interesting and you can learn a lot about cooking.

2 Read the text again. Choose the best answer (a–d) to the questions.

1 The students at the school:

  a have to work in the school garden.

  (b) get some free food for working in the garden.

  c have food science lessons during the holidays.

  d use the vegetables from the garden in cookery lessons.

2 The person who wrote about the school garden:

  a works there with her parents.

  b also helps in her parents' garden.

  c would like to work there in the summer but can't.

  d doesn't have a garden at home.

3 We know that the boy who writes about the farm in Wales definitely:

  a goes there every year.

  b helps on the farm.

  c likes eating meat from the farm.

  d eats only healthy food.

4 The Pink Pig Farm Shop:

  a is the best farm shop in Lincoln.

  b is famous all over Britain.

  c sells only vegetarian food.

  d only sells food from their farm.

5 If you go to the Pink Pig Farm food festival you:

  a have to pay for the food.

  b can watch how to cook different dishes.

  c see animals from the farm.

  d have to take food to sell.

Word Builder Confusing words

3 Complete the sentences with the words below.

> dish food ~~meal~~ snack

1 My favourite ___*meal*___ is breakfast.

2 I take a _____ to school, usually crisps.

3 We always try to eat healthy _____ .

4 Dad made a lovely Mexican _____ using beef, onions and hot chillies.

> dishes food meals snacks

5 Don't eat too many _____ . You won't eat your dinner.

6 The _____ in this shop is always fresh.

7 We have three _____ a day; breakfast, lunch and dinner.

8 There are some interesting _____ from all over the world in this cookery book.

Sentence Builder *because/because of*

4 Choose the correct words to complete the sentences.

1 I like this restaurant (because)/because of the waiters are very friendly.
2 I have to work hard because/because of my exams next week.
3 I didn't sleep because/because of the loud music from the house next door.
4 My dad speaks good French because/because of his dad was French.
5 I eat vegetables because/because of they are healthy.
6 We shop at the supermarket because/because of the low prices.
7 The farm shop is popular because/because of their food is very good.
8 I didn't like the bolognaise because/because of the mushrooms that they put in it.

5 Match the beginnings with the correct endings.

1 I like this café because _b_   a their great cakes.
2 I like this café because of _a_   b their cakes are great.
3 I'm unhealthy because ___   c I eat too many crisps.
4 I'm unhealthy because of ___   d all the crisps I eat.
5 I was angry because of ___   e my brother took my new CD.
6 I was angry because ___   f my brother.
7 Our teacher stopped the lesson because ___   g we were too noisy.
8 Our teacher stopped the lesson because of ___ h the noise.
9 I love Italy because ___   i the people.
10 I love Italy because of ___   j the people are very friendly.

6 Match the questions (1–6) with the answers (a–g). One question has got two answers.

1 How much coffee do you drink?   _d_
2 Do you ever eat fast food?   ___
3 How often do you cook dinner?   ___
4 What is your favourite snack when you're watching a film?   ___
5 Why do you like Italian food?   ___
6 Where do you eat when you are with your friends?   ___

a Once or twice a month but I'm not very good at it.
b Because I love pasta.
c Usually at the pizza restaurant.
d About two cups a day.
e Crisps at home but popcorn at the cinema.
f Yes, every Saturday.
g Because of the fresh meat and vegetables they use.

7 Use the cues to make answers for the questions.

1 Why don't you eat meat?
I / not eat meat / I not want / to eat animals
I don't eat meat because I don't want to eat animals.

2 Why do you and your family eat a lot of vegetables?
We eat / lot / vegetables / we grow them in our garden

_____

3 Why do you like this shop's sandwiches?
I like their sandwiches / the fresh bread they use

_____

4 Why can't you read the menu?
I can't read the menu / I can't speak French

_____

5 Why can't you sleep?
I can't sleep / all the coffee I drank

_____

6 Why do you like these burgers?
I like these burgers / the organic beef

_____

7 Why do you have to go home?
I have / go home / it / be late

_____

8 Why do you like going to the cinema?
I like / go / to the cinema / the popcorn

_____

GRAMMAR
Present Conditional

① * Match the beginnings (1-6) with the correct endings (a-f).

1 If you drink a lot of coffee _____c_____

2 I eat chocolate _____

3 It is dangerous _____

4 If people haven't got much time _____

5 People at my school eat sandwiches _____

6 If you get up late _____

a if you don't cook chicken well.

b if they don't like school dinners.

c you can't sleep.

d they often eat fast food.

e you don't have time for breakfast.

f when I feel sad.

② * Complete the sentences with the correct form of the verbs in brackets.

1 If I _____am_____ (be) hungry at school, I _____eat_____ (eat) chocolate.

2 When my mum _____ (be) busy, she _____ (drink) a lot of coffee.

3 When we _____ (have) parties, we _____ (buy) a lot of crisps.

4 I _____ (not eat) popcorn when I _____ (go) to the cinema.

5 When my dad _____ (go) shopping, he always _____ (get) the cheapest food.

6 My brother always _____ (have) a pizza when we _____ (go) to an Italian restaurant.

7 When my sister _____ (make) breakfast, she never _____ (tidy) the kitchen.

8 My grandmother always _____ (put) the milk in the cup first when she _____ (make) a cup of tea.

③ ** Use the cues to make conditional sentences.

1 If I / tired / have / a shower.
If I'm tired, I have a shower.

2 When my dad / hungry / cook / eggs
_____

3 My sister / listen / loud music / when / happy
_____

4 If it / rain / I / not cycle / to school
_____

5 People / not get / money / they / not work
_____

6 If / my mum / not tell / me to tidy my room / I / not do / it
_____

7 If our teacher / angry / she give / us extra homework
_____

8 When we / go / restaurant / my dad always / have / fish and chips
_____
_____

Grammar Alive Talking about rules

④ *** Complete the questions with the correct words. Then write the answer using the words in brackets.

1 What _____do_____ you eat _____if_____ your parents work late?
(bread and cheese)
If my parents work late, I eat bread and cheese.

2 What _____ your teacher do _____ you _____ noisy?
(we have to sit at the front) If _____
_____ .

3 Where _____ your mum go _____ she wants to relax?
(the garden) When _____
_____ .

4 Who _____ you talk to _____ you feel sad?
(my friends) If _____
_____ .

5 _____ your dad wants to eat out, where _____ he usually go?
(Italian restaurant) My dad _____
_____ .

6 If you _____ know the answer to a question, _____ you ask your teacher?
(No) If _____
_____ .

Speaking Workshop 8

Talk Builder At a café

1 Choose the correct words to complete the sentences.

1 Can I *help*/*serve* you?
2 Here's the *menu/order*.
3 What *do/would* you like?
4 What have you got for *lunch/eat*?
5 I'd *like/want* chicken, please.
6 *For me/Give me*, a burger, please.
7 How *much/price* is that?
8 *Please/Here* you are.

2 Complete the dialogue with the words below.

breakfast ~~can~~ drink here like menu much
sorry thank that's would

Waiter: Good afternoon. ¹____Can____ I help you?
Man: Yes. What have you got for ²_____ ?
Waiter: Here's the ³_____ . I'm ⁴_____ but there are no eggs.
Man: Oh, right.
Waiter: What ⁵_____ you like?
Man: I'd ⁶_____ cereal, please.
Waiter: What would you like to ⁷_____ ?
Man: Coffee, please. How ⁸_____ is that?
Waiter: ⁹_____ £3.50.
Man: ¹⁰_____ you are.
Waiter: ¹¹_____ you.

3 〔51〕 Put the dialogue into the correct order. Listen to check.

a **Waiter:** Good evening, can I help you? _1_
b **Waiter:** Here's the menu. ___
c **Hilary:** I'd like chicken, please. ___
d **Hilary:** Oh dear. Have you got any fish? ___
e **William:** Thank you. ___
f **Waiter:** I'm sorry but there's no chicken. ___
g **William:** Yes. what have you got for dinner? ___
h **Waiter:** What would you like? ___
i **Waiter:** Yes, we've got salmon. ___
j **Hilary:** Okay. I'd like salmon and rice with a salad, please. ___

4 〔52〕 Use the cues to complete the second half of the dialogue. Listen to check.

Waiter: And for you?
William: ¹me / vegetarian pasta
William: *For me, a vegetarian pasta, please.*
Waiter: ²What / like / drink?
Waiter: _____
Hilary: A bottle of water, please.
William: A cola for me, please. ³much / that?
William: _____
Waiter: ⁴£18.80
Waiter: _____
William: ⁵Here
William: _____
Waiter: Thank you.

Exam Choice 4

Reading

1 Read about three restaurants. Match the headings (1-4) with the correct paragraphs (A-C). There is one extra heading.

1 Special food from around the world. ____
2 Fresh food for all the family. ____
3 Vegetarian food with a difference. ____
4 A quick, tasty meal at a great price. ____

A

FARMHOUSE RESTAURANT

Our new restaurant is now open for lunch from 1 p.m.–5 p.m. every day. The restaurant is small and very popular so, you have to reserve a table. We offer two dishes every day using beef, lamb, pork or chicken from our farm. The Farmhouse restaurant is a great place for a relaxed lunch and there is a play area for children to stop them getting bored.

2 Read the text again. Match the people (1-4) with the restaurants that are best for them (A-C). There is one extra person.

1 Greg is quite rich and wants to take his wife somewhere special on Saturday evening to celebrate her fortieth birthday. ____
2 Nigel is a businessman. This Wednesday some Japanese businessmen are coming to his office for a meeting. He wants to take them somewhere nice for lunch. ____
3 Helen has got a three-year-old son. She needs to go shopping tomorrow and wants to take her son with her and have lunch and a rest. ____
4 Ellen works in an office. She only gets half an hour for lunch and needs to find some food to eat quickly or to take back to the office. ____

Listening

3 🔊53 Listen to someone talking about food. Match her answers (1-5) with the topics below (a-f). There is one extra topic.

a the international food she likes best ____
b how often she goes to restaurants ____
c how good she is at cooking ____
d how healthy her eating habits are ____
e her favourite restaurant ____
f the food she doesn't like ____

B

The Look Out

We are an all-day café serving hot and cold snacks at low prices. Sandwiches, pizza, burgers, eggs and salads, hot and cold drinks. It's quick, it's clean, it's cheap and it's friendly. Eat in the café or take your food away.

We are open Monday–Saturday, 8 a.m.–6 p.m.

C

The Palace

The Palace restaurant is in a beautiful building next to the park gates. It is open for dinner every day from 6 p.m. until 11 p.m. and, at the weekends it also offers lunch from one o'clock. We use only the best food and the restaurant is perfect for romantic evenings as it is very quiet. We have Italian, French, Mexican, Egyptian, Chinese and Japanese food from only £30 per person.

Speaking

4 Complete the dialogue with the correct words or phrases a, b or c.

Waiter:	Can I ¹____ you?
Adam:	Yes, please. We'd like dinner.
Waiter:	²____ the menu.
Adam:	Thank you. Oh, salmon. I love salmon.
Alice:	³____ !
Adam:	But it's quite expensive.
Alice:	⁴____ . I haven't got much money.
Adam:	⁵____ . We could have pasta with vegetables.
Alice:	Good idea.
Waiter:	What ⁶____ to eat?
Adam:	We'd like the pasta with broccoli, please.
Waiter:	⁷____ . We haven't got any broccoli. We've got cabbage.
Alice:	Oh no, not cabbage. I don't like ⁸____ .
Adam:	We'll have pasta and mushrooms, please.

1 a help   b give   c serve
2 a There's   b Where's   c Here's
3 a Me too   b That's true   c Me neither
4 a I like it b That's true   c Me too
5 a Me too   b Here you are   c Me neither
6 a do you like b would you like c will you like
7 a That's true b Here you are   c I'm sorry
8 a it   b to   c him

90

Use of English

5 **Choose the correct replies.**

1 Are you going to learn French next year?
  a Yes, I am.
  b Yes, I do.
  c Yes, I'm going.

2 Would you like some water?
  a Yes, I do.
  b Yes, I like it.
  c Yes, I would.

3 Did you like the film?
  a No, I was boring.
  b No, I was bored.
  c No, it was bored.

4 What do you have to do at home?
  a I play computer games and watch TV.
  b I have to tidy my room.
  c I've got a computer and a CD player.

5 Will I get married?
  a No, you won't.
  b No, you don't.
  c No, you aren't.

6 What do you do when you are tired?
  a I'll go to bed.
  b I go to bed.
  c I'd like to go to bed.

6 **Complete the text with the correct words.**

Dear Paul,

I'm going ¹_____ go to the cinema with my friends soon and then we're going to have something to eat. Do you want to come? There's a new Chinese restaurant next to the cinema. When people come out of the cinema, they ²_____ often hungry so I'm sure it ³_____ be busy.

When we go to the cinema, we're ⁴_____ going to eat any popcorn. We're ⁵_____ to wait so that we are really hungry when we get to the restaurant ⁶_____ we love Chinese food.

I ⁷_____ to be home by ten o'clock so I hope the waiters work quickly! I don't want to leave half of my dinner because ⁸_____ the time!

I don't know what films will be on next week. I'd ⁹_____ to see a Pixar animation. My friends and I like them a lot.

Writing

7 **Choose the best phrases for a formal email.**

1 *Hi there .../Dear Sir, Madam ...*
2 *Can you give me some information about .../I am writing to ask for information about ...*
3 *I want to know .../I'd like to know ...*
4 *I would also like .../And I'd like ...*
5 *I look forward to hearing from you./Write soon.*
6 *Yours/Yours faithfully*

8 **You see a poster giving details of a competition. Write an email asking for more information.**

Epping Cookery
Competition

Are you between fifteen and nineteen years old?

Can you cook?

Would you like to become 'Epping's Young Cook of the Year'?

The Forest Restaurant is holding a competition to find the best local chefs. Win a free meal at our restaurant for four people.

For more information, contact Eppcook@forest.com

- Say why you are writing and give some personal information
- Ask questions: When? / What food?
- Ask more questions: have to pay to enter the competition?

Check Your Progress 8

1 Food **Complete the words with the correct letters.**

1 I love fruit. My favourite are a __ __ l __ s .
2 I don't eat many vegetables but I like
  c __ __ __ o __ __ and p __ __ __ t __ __ __ __ .
3 I eat a lot of cereals like p __ __ t __ .
4 My favourite meat is l __ __ __ and b __ __ __ .
5 Fish is very good for you so I eat a lot of
  s __ __ d __ n __ __ and t __ __ __ .
6 I eat a y __ __ h __ __ __ every morning and this
  dairy food is good for me.
7 When I want a snack, I have some n __ t __ .

/10

2 Predictions *will/won't* **Use the cues to complete the questions and answers.**

1 next year / be easy?

   _____

2 no / not. next year / very difficult

   _____

3 we have / lots of tests?

   _____

4 yes / . We / have tests every week

   _____

5 we go / on / lot of school trips?

   _____

6 no / not. we / not have time

   _____

7 which teachers / we have

   _____

8 we / not know / until September

   _____

/8

3 Present Conditional **Complete the sentences with the correct forms of the verbs in brackets.**

1 If people _____ (not have) a lot of money,
  they _____ (not often eat) at restaurants.
2 When my dad _____ (be) hungry, he
  _____ (buy) crisps from the local shop.
3 What _____ (your mum do) when she
  _____ (feel) tired?
4 I _____ (not go) out when I _____
  (have) exams at school.
5 _____ (you drink) cola when you
  _____ (meet) your friends?
6 When my sister _____ (lose) her phone,
  she _____ (get) very angry.
7 When our teacher _____ (not give) us
  homework, we _____ (be) very happy.
8 If I _____ (not eat) breakfast, I
  _____ (not study) well.

/8

4 At a café **Match the beginnings (1-9) with the endings (a-i)**

1 Hello, can I ____
2 What have you got ____
3 Here's the ____
4 I'm sorry, there's ____
5 What would ____
6 A coffee for ____
7 How much ____
8 That's ____
9 Here ____

a menu.
b £10.80, please.
c me, please.
d no chicken.
e you are.
f you like to drink?
g for lunch?
h is that?
i help you?

/9

TOTAL SCORE   */35*

Module Diary 8

1 **Look at the objectives on page 81 in the Students' Book. Choose three and evaluate your learning.**

1 Now I can _____ well / quite well /
  with problems.
2 Now I can _____ well / quite well /
  with problems.
3 Now I can _____ well / quite well /
  with problems.

2 **Look at your results. What language areas in this module do you need to study more?**

TOPIC TALK - VOCABULARY

1 Complete the text with the correct words. You can see the first letter of each word.

There are four ¹ _seasons_ in a year. The coldest is ²w_____ . In a lot of countries in Europe it snows and skiing is very popular. Next comes ³s_____ when the weather gets warmer and flowers start to grow. The hottest time of the year is ⁴s_____ . A lot of people go to the beach. Finally, there is ⁵a_____ . The trees turn into beautiful colours – reds, yellows and browns and it starts getting colder again.

2 Complete the words with the correct letters.

1 c _l o u d y_

2 c _ _ _ _

3 r _ _ _ _ _

4 s _ _ w _

5 f _ _ g _

6 w _ _ _ _ _

7 s _ n _ _

8 h _ _

3 Label the picture with the words below.

centre   east   ~~north~~   south   west

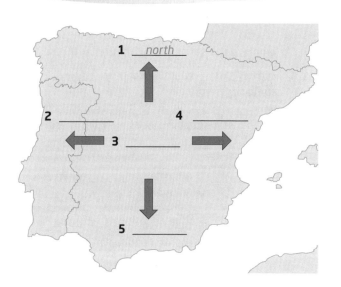

1 _north_

2 _____

3 _____

4 _____

5 _____

4 Match the beginnings (1-8) with the correct endings (a-h).

1 My country is   _d_

2 The population is   ___

3 Our capital city   ___

4 In the summer   ___

5 In the winter   ___

6 In the north, there   ___

7 There are twenty-three national   ___

8 The biggest mountain is   ___

a is in the centre of the country.

b a lot of people go skiing.

c are some beautiful beaches.

d quite big.

e parks.

f it is hot but it can be rainy.

g 2499 metres high.

h forty million.

GRAMMAR
a/an/the

❶ * Complete the sentences with *a* or *an*.

1 I am __*a*__ student at __*a*__ language school.

2 I usually eat ___ apple for lunch.

3 We have to write ___ essay for English.

4 Do you play ___ musical instrument?

5 I wrote ___ email to my friend in France.

6 There is ___ sofa and ___ armchair in the living room.

7 My dad's ___ engineer and my mum's ___ vet.

8 I've got ___ summer job as ___ waiter.

❷ ** Complete the sentences with *a/an* or *the*.

1 I live in __*a*__ beautiful country. __*The*__ capital city is very old.

2 I am _____ teacher in _____ very big school. _____ students in my class work very hard.

3 I live in _____ small house. There is no dining room so we eat in _____ kitchen.

4 There's _____ art gallery, _____ theatre and there are two cinemas in my town. _____ theatre and _____ art gallery are very modern but _____ cinemas are old.

5 I saw _____ great skirt and top in _____ shop in _____ town centre. _____ skirt was cheap but _____ top was very expensive.

6 I went to see _____ film last night. _____ acting was very good.

7 I go to school by bus. _____ bus is often late.

8 I'm going to have _____ party next Saturday. It's going to be _____ best party ever!

❸ ** Complete the sentences with the phrases below.

> at (x 3)   at a (x 2)   ~~at the~~   for   for the   go to
> go to the   have (x 2)   have a

1 My dad is ___*at*___ work, my mum's ___*at*___ home and my brother is ___*at the*___ new swimming pool in Park Street.

2 What time do you _____ breakfast?

3 Steve and Mary _____ cinema every Friday.

4 We usually have pizza _____ lunch.

5 Do you _____ lunch _____ school?

6 Does your dad _____ shower in the morning?

7 My mum made cakes _____ people at her work.

8 My parents often eat _____ restaurant.

9 I _____ school by bus.

10 Chris is _____ party.

❹ * Complete the dialogue with *a, an, the* or no article (-).**

Jackie: Hi, James. Where are you?

James: I'm at [1]_____-_____ home. Why?

Jackie: I need help. You know [2]_____ essay we have to do for geography? I don't know what to write.

James: Which essay?

Jackie: [3]_____ one about [4]_____ climate of North America.

James: Oh that. I know [5]_____ good website. I'll send you [6]_____ email with [7]_____ address.

Jackie: Great, thanks. What are you doing later?

James: Nothing. Why?

Jackie: I'm going to get [8]_____ pizza for [9]_____ lunch. Do you want to come?

James: Where?

Jackie: To [10]_____ pizza restaurant in Chapel Street. [11]_____ pizzas there are great.

James: Okay. What time?

Jackie: Let's meet at two o'clock.

James: I'll be there. I'll send [12]_____ email now. Bye.

Jackie: Bye. Thanks.

5 ** The sentences below don't have *a*, *an* or *the*. Put them in the correct places.

1 We watched ⌃ film in English today. _____*a film*_____

2 This is great gym. _____

3 I have lunch at school. Food at our school is very good. _____

4 Dad's at work. He's at meeting. _____

5 That was fantastic film. Who was director? _____ , _____

6 Let's eat at café next to cinema. _____ , _____

7 Be quiet! Class 5C are doing exam. _____

8 Have you got lot of friends at university? _____

9 There is new bookshop in town centre. _____ , _____

6 *** Choose the correct answers.

1 Was Paul _*a*_ school today?
  a at   **b** at the   **c** at a

2 Our homework is to write ___ essay on sport.
  a the   **b** -   **c** an

3 What do you want for ___ lunch?
  a a   **b** -   **c** the

4 We went to the town centre ___ bus.
  a by the   **b** by   **c** by a

5 What's ___ population of America?
  a the   **b** -   **c** a

6 Steve's at ___ meeting.
  a a   **b** the   **c** -

7 I don't want to go ___ home.
  a to   **b** -   **c** to the

8 I want to go to Spain in ___ summer.
  a a   **b** -   **c** the

9 I want to have ___ shower before we go out.
  a the   **b** a   **c** -

10 We stayed in a hotel on ___ coast.
  a -   **b** the   **c** a

Grammar Alive Asking about places

7 *** Erin is a new student at a school in London. Complete her questions about the school and the responses.

1 **A:** computer classroom?
  B: ✓ but computers / old
  A: *Is there a computer classroom?* _____
  B: *Yes, there is but the computers are old.* _____

2 **A:** shop?
  B: ✓ but / snacks there / very expensive
  A: _____
  B: _____

3 **A:** teachers nice?
  B: ✓ nicer than / teachers / my old school
  A: _____
  B: _____

4 **A:** library?
  B: ✓ and librarian very helpful
  A: _____
  B: _____

5 **A:** film club?
  B: ✗ but good cinema near school
  A: _____
  B: _____

6 **A:** drama club?
  B: ✗ was last year but drama teacher left in summer holidays.
  A: _____
  B: _____

SKILLS
Reading

1 Read some suggestions about visiting the Dominican Republic. Tick (✓) the five things that the people talk about and cross (✗) the three that they don't talk about.

1 National parks   ✗
2 The climate
3 Clothes to wear
4 Animals and birds
5 A town to visit
6 Good hotels to stay in
7 A festival
8 Something to eat

What Holiday Forum

Page 1 of 3   1 2 3

Richard_108
1040 posts

Dominican Republic?

Hi, I'm planning a trip to the Dominican Republic later this year. I'd love to know where to go, what to see, etc. Any ideas welcome. Richard

posted on 15 Feb

sunshine90
130 posts

Hi Richard
You'll have a great time. The Dominican Republic is beautiful. Go to Jarabacoa. It's got a great climate. The temperature is between 16° and 22°C all year. That's why a lot of people call it 'The Everlasting Spring' because it's always spring time there. There's a great festival in February with music and dancing and it's close to Pico Duarte the highest mountain in the Caribbean. It's 3,098 metres high but you can walk to the top. It takes about three days and you have to go with someone who knows the area. There are places to sleep on the mountain but you need warm clothes because it's very cold at night.

posted on 16 Feb

Fred_dilling
16 posts

Hi Richard,
If you like history, spend a few days in the capital, Santo Domingo. Columbus came here in 1492 and there are a lot of beautiful old buildings. It's a big city – two million people live here so there is a lot to do. Come between February and April. That's the 'dry' season (but bring a coat because it's always rainy here!) Try the local food. The best is La Bandera. It is meat, red beans and rice. It's lovely!

posted on 19 Feb

2 Read the text again and complete the notes.

Jarabacoa
Temperature: From ¹ _____16°C_____
            to ² _____
People often call it: ³ _____

Pico Duarte
How high: ⁴ _____ metres
Time you need
to walk to the top: ⁵ _____

Santo Domingo
Population: ⁶ _____
Things to see: ⁷ _____

Other things
Best time to come to
the Dominican Republic: ⁸ _____
Food and drink: La Bandera is a dish
               of ⁹ _____

Word Builder Nationality adjectives

3 Complete the text with the correct form of the words in brackets.

There are a lot of people in my English class from all over the world. There are three ¹ _Spanish_ (Spain) girls, two ² _____ (Turkey) boys, four ³ _____ (Poland) students, three ⁴ _____ (Japan) students and a ⁵ _____ (China) girl. There was a ⁶ _____ (Greece) boy but he left. I think a ⁷ _____ (France) girl is going to start next week.

Last year, we had an ⁸ _____ (America) teacher. No, sorry, he was from Toronto so he was ⁹ _____ (Canada). Now, we've got a ¹⁰ _____ (Britain) woman. She's very nice. Her name's Carole.

Listening

4 🔈54 Listen to the conversation and answer the questions about Nicola's holiday.

1 When did she arrive home from her holiday?
Last night.

2 Where did she stay in The Dominican Republic?
In _____

3 How long was she there for?
For _____

4 What animals did she see?
She saw _____ , _____ and
_____ .

5 What food did she eat?
_____

6 How many days with no rain were there?
There were _____ without rain.

7 Where are her photos?
They are on her _____ .

5 🔈54 Listen again. Match the people (Matt and Nicola) with the sentences. Write M (Matt) or N (Nicola).

Who:

1 wants to know about the other person's holiday? _M_

2 is confused about two countries with similar names? ____

3 didn't do something he/she wanted to do? ____

4 hears about an animal for the first time during the conversation? ____

5 has stopped eating something that he/she likes? ____

6 has to go somewhere? ____

someone, anyone, everyone, no one

❶ * **Choose the correct words to complete the sentences.**

1 We won't spend much money. There's ~~nothing~~/ anything to buy.

2 *No one/Anyone* knows where we are.

3 Is there *anyone/anywhere* waiting for you?

4 I don't want to go *nowhere/anywhere* this evening.

5 Where did you go? *Anywhere/Nowhere* special.

6 I haven't got *anything/nothing* to wear.

7 I looked *anywhere/everywhere* but I couldn't find my phone.

8 We've seen *something/everything* here. Let's go *somewhere/anywhere* else.

9 Is *someone/everyone* here? Good, let's go.

10 I met *anyone/someone* from my old primary school.

❷ ** **Complete the dialogue with the words below. There are three extra words.**

> anyone   anything   ~~anywhere~~   everyone
> everything   everywhere   no one   nothing
> nowhere   something   somewhere

A: What are you doing?

B: I'm organising my summer holidays.

A: Oh. Are you going ¹ _anywhere_ special?

B: Yes, I'm going ² _____ new this year. Bulgaria.

A: Are you going with ³ _____ ?

B: No. ⁴ _____ I know wants to go. They think it's cold and there's ⁵ _____ to do but the Black Sea is beautiful and there are some lovely towns and villages. Hey, would you like to come?

A: Yes, of course.

B: I'll give you ⁶ _____ to read then you'll know where you want to go.

A: Great. Wow, Bulgaria. I know where I want to go.

B: Where?

A: ⁷ _____ ! I want to see ⁸ _____ !

B: Well, I'm only going for two weeks but we'll do our best.

Grammar Alive Suggestions

❸ ** **Use the cues to make suggestions and negative replies. Use *something*, *somewhere* or *someone* in the suggestions and *nothing*, *no one* or *nowhere*.**

1 go / tonight
to go
Let's go somewhere tonight.
There's nowhere to go.

2 watch / at the cinema
good on
_____
_____

3 cook / for dinner
in the fridge
_____
_____

4 ask / for a dance
I want to dance with
_____
_____

❹ *** **Use the cues to make dialogues. Use the words in brackets.**

1 (something)
A: want / eat / healthy?
B: No, / eat / nice but unhealthy
A: *Do you want to eat something healthy?*
B: *No, I want to eat something nice but unhealthy.*

2 (somewhere)
A: want / go / hot this summer?
B: No, / go / cool
A: _____
B: _____

3 (anyone)
A: going to invite / from your Saturday job / your party?
B: No, they won't know / from school
A: _____
B: _____

4 (something)
A: want / to drink?
B: Yes, please. like / cold
A: _____
B: _____

5 (anything / nothing / something)
A: have got / to eat?
B: No, I / got / . Let's get / in this café
A: _____
B: _____

Speaking Workshop 9

1 **Complete the sentences with the correct words.**

[1]C_ross_____ the road when you get to the bank and then [2]t_____ left. Go [3]p_____ the supermarket and turn [4]r_____ . Go [5]a_____ the street for about 200 metres and you'll see the cinema in [6]f_____ of you.

2 **Complete the dialogue with the words and phrases below.**

> excuse me   from here   go along   past
> how do you get   in front   next to
> the street   you'll see

A: [1]_Excuse me,_ do you know the City School?

B: Yes, I do.

A: [2]_____ to it [3]_____ ?

B: [4]_____ this street for about 500 metres. Go [5]_____ the station and [6]_____ a restaurant [7]_____ of you. When you get to the restaurant, cross [8]_____ and turn left. The City School is on the left. It's [9]_____ a supermarket.

3 **55** **Complete the dialogue with the with questions and phrases (a–g). Then listen to check.**

Sean: Excuse me.
       [1]_Do you know the Green Parrot café?_____

Zoe: Yes,

Sean: [2]_____

Zoe: Erm … Cross the street. Turn right …
       Go past the cinema, and then turn left.

Sean: Okay. Cross the street. Go past the cinema.
       [3]_____

Zoe: No, no. Turn left. Go along the street …
       [4]_____ Oh no, that's The Blue Moon café … [5]_____ … Sorry!

Sean: Excuse me. I'm looking for the Green Parrot café. [6]_____

Jim: The Green Parrot? Sorry, mate. No idea.
       [7]_____

a How do you get to it from here?

b Ask somebody else!

c And then you'll see it on your right.

d Do you know the Green Parrot café?

e Do you know it?

f Oh I don't know

g Turn right.

4 **56** **Put the next part of the dialogue in the correct order. Then listen to check.**

a **Sean:**   East London! I don't know this area of London. And you?

b **Sean:**   Great! Thanks a lot.

c **Sean:**   Sorry, can you repeat that please?

d **Sean:**   That's right! How do you get there from here?

e **Bob:**   Where are you from?

f **Bob:**   Go along this street for about a hundred metres. You'll see the station in front of you, and The Green Parrot is next to it.

g **Bob:**   It's this way. You cross the street, turn left, then … I'm going that way, too. I can show you!

h **Bob:**   I'm not from London but I've got a good map! I'm stopping here, but go along this street for about a hundred metres. You'll see the station in front of you, and The Green Parrot is next to it.

i **Bob:**   Yes, I do. It's an internet café.

   Sean: Excuse me. Do you know The Green Parrot café?

1 _Bob: Yes I do. It's an internet café._____

2 _____

3 _____

4 _____

5 _____

6 _____

7 _____

8 _____

Sean: Thanks. Brilliant.

Writing Workshop 5

Sentence Builder *to* for purpose

1 **Match the beginnings (1-7) with the correct endings (a-g).**

1 I'm going to the beach   _c_
2 I've got a camera   ___
3 We went to a restaurant   ___
4 I phoned my friend   ___
5 I went onto the internet   ___
6 We went to the cinema   ___
7 My parents are going shopping   ___

a to have a birthday dinner.
b to look at information about Costa Rica.
c to swim.
d to get some food for dinner.
e to see the new James Bond film.
f to take photos of the animals.
g to tell him about my holiday.

2 **Complete the sentences with the correct form of the verbs below.**

ask   change   contact   listen   play
read   ~~see~~   sleep

1 We went to Paris ___*to see*___ the Eiffel Tower.
2 We went to the bank _____ our pounds into Euros.
3 We stopped a man in the street _____ for directions.
4 We took a tent _____ in.
5 We took our phones _____ our parents.
6 Rob took three books _____ on the beach.
7 Dan took his MP3 player _____ to on the bus.
8 Steve took his guitar _____ in the evenings.

3 **Look at the postcard. Put the information (a-e) in the correct order.**

a What he is going to do after tomorrow.   ___
b What he did yesterday   ___
c Where he is and a description of it.   _1_
d What he is going to do tomorrow   ___
e Why he likes the place   ___

Hi Tom,

I'm in Sorrento. It's a beautiful city next to the sea. Yesterday, we went to a 'gelato' bar to eat one of their forty-eight kinds of ice cream! Then we got on a train to go to Pompeii. It's amazing. I bought a book about it to learn more about what happened. Tomorrow, I'm going there again not to see the Roman city but to get the bus to Vesuvius. Then on Wednesday, I'm going to Capri to see 'the most beautiful island in the world'. That's what people say. I love it here. The people are friendly, the food is excellent and the weather is perfect.

See you soon,

Mike

---

4 **Use the cues to write a postcard from Meersburg in Germany.**

Dear Mel,

1 I / now / Meersburg
I'm now in Meersburg. _____

2 it / beautiful / town / next / lake
_____

3 Yesterday, we go / 'island garden' of Mainau
_____

4 it / very beautiful. we / have great time
_____

5 this morning / dad / buy / video camera
_____

6 Later / we go / on boat to Switzerland
_____

7 Dad want / film / lake and mountains
_____

8 like / here / very relaxing / quiet.
_____

See you soon
Elaine

Sound Choice 5

Sound Check

Say the words and expressions below.

a a computer, an apple, the cinema, the airport (Exercise 1)

b We'll go, They'd like, I'll be (Exercise 2)

c the, there, then (Exercise 3)

d north, go, phone, walk (Exercise 4)

e right, caught, bought (Exercise 5)

f Do you know the Park Hotel? Can I help you? How do you get to it from here? (Exercise 6)

g biscuits, juice, fruit (Exercise 7)

57 **Listen and check your answers. Which sounds and expressions did you have problems with? Choose three exercises to do below.**

1a **58** Grammar – Articles **Listen to the articles and write (V) if the next word starts with a vowel or (C) if it starts with a consonant.**

1 _V_ **3** __ **5** __ **7** __
2 __ **4** __ **6** __ **8** __

1b **59** Grammar – Articles **Now listen to check your answers to Exercise 1a.**

2 **60** Contractions **Listen to the sentences and tick (✓) the words you hear.**

1 We'd ☐ We'll ✓ We ☐
2 They'd ☐ They'll ☐ They ☐
3 I'd ☐ I'll ☐ I ☐
4 You'd ☐ You'll ☐ You ☐
5 He'd ☐ He'll ☐ He ☐
6 She'd ☐ She'll ☐ She ☐

3 **61** Consonants **Listen and repeat the words.**

the these
there mother
then brother
this father
that

4 **62** Vowels **Listen to the words below. Write them in the correct group depending on their vowel sounds.**

~~north~~ go phone walk snow shorts bored coast

/ɔː/ saw	/əʊ/ know
north	__
__	__
__	__
__	__

5 **63** Spelling **Listen and write the words. Write the number of letters in each word.**

1 _right (5)_ **6** __
2 __ **7** __
3 __ **8** __
4 __ **9** __
5 __ **10** __

6 **64** Expressions **Listen and repeat the questions. Tick (✓) the two which are said by a waiter.**

1 Do you know the Park Hotel? ☐
2 What have you got for lunch? ☐
3 Can I help you? ☐
4 How much is that? ☐
5 What would you like to drink? ☐
6 How do you get to it from here? ☐

7 **65** Difficult words **Listen to the words and answer the questions.**

1 biscuits, juice, fruit
Which word has a different sound for the letters 'ui'?
biscuits

2 salmon, yoghurt, lamb
Which word has a silent letter at the end of the word?
__

3 favourite, cucumber, strawberry
Which word has three syllables?
__

4 lettuce, lunch, yoghurt
Which word has an /ɪ/ sound for the letter 'u'?
__

5 bread, cereal, beans
Which word has two separate sounds for the letters 'ea'?
__

Check Your Progress 9

1 Countries **Complete the sentences with the correct words. You can see the first letter of each word.**

1 My favourite s_____ is spring because it is so beautiful.
2 The c_____ of Britain is London.
3 The p_____ of the USA is about 300 million.
4 The w_____ is not very nice today – it's rainy and cold.
5 There are eight n_____ p_____ in our country full of animals and plants.
6 I live in the n_____ of the country but the biggest cities are in the south.
7 The highest m_____ is 4200metres high.
8 Our country has a very nice climate. It isn't too hot in the s_____ and it isn't too cold in the w_____ .

/9

2 *a, an, the, -* **Complete the text with *a, an, the* or –.**

This country is in Europe. It is ¹_____ big country. ²_____ capital is in the centre of ³_____ country and the population is about fort-six million.

The people have ⁴_____ lunch in the afternoon. It is the biggest meal of the day. They usually eat at ⁵_____ home but, in big cities, they can't always do this. They often have ⁶_____ snack before dinner because they have ⁷_____ dinner quite late, at 9 p.m. or later. ⁸_____ snack is called 'La Merienda'. They often eat ⁹_____ bread with ham or cheese. What is the country? Spain.

/9

3 Nationalities **Make nationalities from the countries below and put them in the correct column of the table.**

America   Britain   Canada   China   France
Greece   Japan   Poland   Spain   Turkey

-an	-ish	-ese	other endings
___	___	___	___
___	___	___	___
	___		
	___		

/10

4 *someone, everyone, anyone, no one* **Complete the sentences with the correct words.**

1 I want to go _____ nice this summer.
2 We woke up in the middle of the night and heard _____ walking around in the living room.
3 I'm bored. I haven't got _____ to talk to.
4 My phone rang but, when I answered, there was _____ there.
5 There's _____ important I want to tell you.
6 They didn't have vegetarian food so I didn't have _____ to eat.
7 My first day of school was great. _____ was very kind.

/7

TOTAL SCORE   /35

Module Diary 9

1 **Look at the objectives on page 79 in the Students' Book. Choose three and evaluate your learning.**

1 Now I can _____ well / quite well / with problems.
2 Now I can _____ well / quite well / with problems.
3 Now I can _____ well / quite well / with problems.

2 **Look at your results. What language areas in this module do you need to study more?**

TOPIC TALK – VOCABULARY

1 Match the beginnings (1-8) with the correct endings (a-h).

1 I never buy   _c_
2 Dad's checking his   ___
3 My brother often downloads   ___
4 Something's happened. I can't go   ___
5 You spend too much time playing   ___
6 Please read my   ___
7 Don't phone your friend in America. It's much cheaper to use   ___
8 When I come home from holiday, the first thing I do is to upload my   ___

a online.
b blog.
c things online.
d photos to the internet.
e Skype.
f emails.
g online games.
h music from the internet.

2 Complete the words. You can see the first letter of the words.

Things I need to buy:

1 d_igital_____ camera

2 e-book r_____

3 DVD p_____

4 new m_____ phone – this time I want a s_____ phone.

5 16GB USB f_____ d_____

6 v_____ camera

7 video game c_____

3 Complete the words with the correct letters.

I've got a [1]d _e s k t o p_ computer in my bedroom. It's very fast and great for playing [2]o __ l __ __ __ computer games. I've also got a [3]l __ __ t __ __ . It's quite old now. I've got photos on it and music. It's good to take to people's houses but I'm going to get a [4]n __ __ b __ __ __ soon which will be smaller and lighter. A lot of my friends have sold their computers and bought [5]t __ b __ __ __ __ but I don't think I'll get one until they are cheaper.

I've also got an MP3 [6]p __ __ y __ __ which I listen to on the bus to school. My parents don't like technology. They've got a new car with [7]S __ __ N __ __ but they don't know how to use it.

4 Complete the dialogue with the words below.

because   favourite gadget   I'd like   into   ~~not~~
often use   sometimes send   so useful

A: Are you interested in technology?
B: No, I'm [1]_____not_____ really [2]_____ it.
A: Do you use it at all?
B: Well, yes. I [3]_____ Facebook and I [4]_____ emails.
A: Have you got a [5]_____ ?
B: Not really. I like my phone [6]_____ it is [7]_____ . It isn't a new phone and it isn't smart or anything like that. I only use it to make phone calls. That's quite strange these days!
A: Is there anything you'd like to have?
B: [8]_____ to have a new TV. A big one.

28 Present Perfect

❶ * Write the 3ʳᵈ form of the verbs.

1 try   *tried*
2 do   _____
3 go   _____
4 buy   _____
5 see   _____
6 have   _____
7 come   _____
8 write   _____
9 take   _____
10 put   _____

❷ * Complete the sentences with the verbs in brackets in the Past Perfect.

1 We *have learned* (learn) a lot about computers at school.
2 I _____ (read) about tablets and I _____ (use) my friend's.
3 My dad _____ (spend) a lot of money on gadgets.
4 My mum _____ (have) three jobs in her life.
5 My brother _____ (buy) a new net book.
6 My friend _____ (start) writing a blog.
7 Students from my class _____ (win) five English competitions.
8 I _____ (write) a lot of emails in my life.
9 Mark _____ (upload) his photos to the internet. Let's look at them.

❸ ** Complete the sentences with the verbs in the box in the correct form.

> send   buy   pass   finish   spend
> lose   start   ~~win~~

1 She *has won* a lot of money and is going to spend it on a holiday.
2 He _____ his homework and he can relax now.
3 He _____ his mobile phone and he doesn't know where it is.
4 They _____ a lot of clothes and haven't got any money left.
5 He _____ all his exams and his parents are very pleased with him.
6 They _____ all their money on computer games.
7 She _____ an email to her friend and is waiting for her friend to write back.
8 I _____ a new job. It's hard work but I like it.

❹ ** Use the cues to make sentences in the Present Perfect.

1 I / buy / a laptop but I / not use / it
I have bought a laptop but I haven't used it.
2 I / write / a blog but I / not upload / any photos to it
_____
3 We / started / the game but we / not finish / it
_____
4 My dad / be / to London but he / not see / Big Ben
_____
5 I / read / my English book but I / not do / my English homework
_____
6 They / have / lunch but they / not have / dinner
_____
7 I / download / some songs but I / not listen / to them
_____

❺ ** Complete the sentences with the verb in capitals in the correct form; Present Simple, Past Simple and Present Perfect.

1 LEARN
a Everyone *learns* maths at school.
b We *learned* a lot last year.
c I *have learned* a lot about Shakespeare in my life.
2 SPEND
d I _____ about £10 a week.
e My parents _____ £100 last weekend.
f Mark _____ all his money.
3 NOT BUY
g My friend has seen a tablet that he likes but he _____ it because he hasn't got any money.
h There's a shop at our school. It sells snacks but I _____ often _____ anything there because it is very expensive.
i We went to the shops but we _____ anything because we didn't see anything we wanted.
4 READ
j I _____ two books last weekend.
k Dan _____ all the time.
l I _____ this book – it's great.

6 *** **Complete the sentences with the verbs below in the Present Perfect with *never*.**

be play send ~~use~~

1 My mum __*has never used*__ Facebook.
2 My dad _____ a text message.
3 My grandfather _____ online.
4 My grandmother _____ a computer game.

hear read try win

5 My sister _____ any Beatles songs.
6 I _____ any books by Charles Dickens.
7 My friends _____ any competitions.
8 My parents _____ Japanese food.

buy learn take upload

9 My mum _____ to drive.
10 My sister _____ any photos with her new camera.
11 I _____ anything online.
12 My friend _____ any photos to the internet.

be read surf want

13 My grandparents _____ the internet.
14 My parents _____ to a rock concert.
15 My brother _____ my blog.
16 I _____ to be an actor.

Grammar Alive Talking about achievements

7 *** **Use the cues to make dialogues about achievements.**

1 **A:** win / competition
   B: Great! I / never / win a competition but I / come second three times.
   A: *I have won a competition.*
   B: *Great! I have never won a competition but I have come second three times.*

2 **A:** read / all of Shakespeare's plays
   B: Wow! I / never read / any / his plays but I / see two at the theatre.
   A: _____
   B: _____

3 **A:** I / be / to America
   B: Really? I / never / be / America but I / be / thirteen countries in Europe
   A: _____
   B: _____

4 **A:** I / start / a Saturday job
   B: I never / have a Saturday job but I / work in the summer holidays
   A: _____
   B: _____

5 **A:** I / buy / the new Adele CD
   B: I / never / buy a CD but I / download / a lot of songs
   A: _____
   B: _____

6 **A:** My grandfather / write a blog
   B: My grandfather / never write / a blog but he / write three books
   A: _____
   B: _____

1 Read the text quickly. Match the headings (a-e) with the paragraphs (1-4). There is one extra heading.

a My behaviour upset other people.
b Things we use the internet for.
c Others control my use.
d Nothing has helped me.
e Useful information and a great feature.

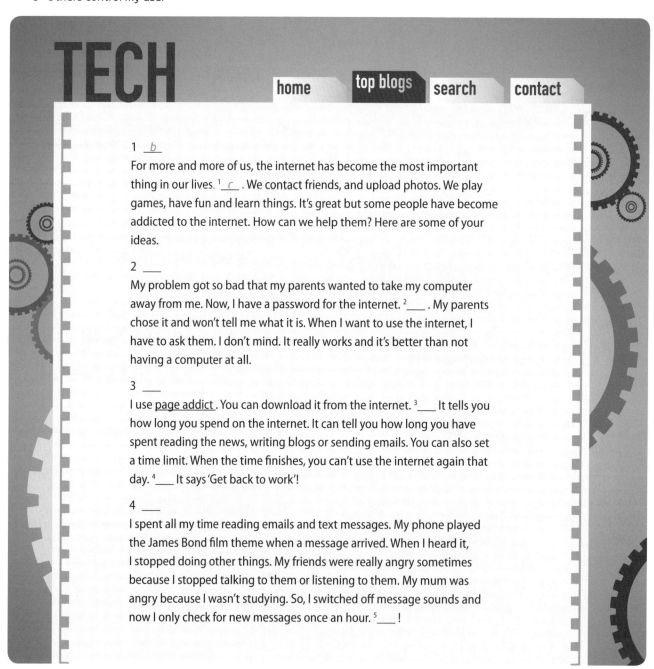

TECH

home | top blogs | search | contact

1 _b_

For more and more of us, the internet has become the most important thing in our lives. [1] _c_ . We contact friends, and upload photos. We play games, have fun and learn things. It's great but some people have become addicted to the internet. How can we help them? Here are some of your ideas.

2 ___

My problem got so bad that my parents wanted to take my computer away from me. Now, I have a password for the internet. [2]___ . My parents chose it and won't tell me what it is. When I want to use the internet, I have to ask them. I don't mind. It really works and it's better than not having a computer at all.

3 ___

I use page addict . You can download it from the internet. [3]___ It tells you how long you spend on the internet. It can tell you how long you have spent reading the news, writing blogs or sending emails. You can also set a time limit. When the time finishes, you can't use the internet again that day. [4]___ It says 'Get back to work'!

4 ___

I spent all my time reading emails and text messages. My phone played the James Bond film theme when a message arrived. When I heard it, I stopped doing other things. My friends were really angry sometimes because I stopped talking to them or listening to them. My mum was angry because I wasn't studying. So, I switched off message sounds and now I only check for new messages once an hour. [5]___ !

2 Read the text again. Match the sentences (a-f) with the gaps in the text (1-5). There is one extra sentence.

a People can wait that long for a reply
b I don't know it.
c We use it for work or study.
d When you try, you see a message.
e They want to stop but they can't
f You don't have to pay anything and it's easy to use.

Word Builder *have*

❸ Match the questions (1-7) with the correct answers (a-g).

1 What sounds do you have on your phone?   _c_
2 How often do you and your friends have parties? ___
3 Are you having a good time in Portugal?   ___
4 What time do you have breakfast?   ___
5 Do you have problems at school because of your phone or computer?   ___
6 Where do you usually have lunch?   ___
7 Do you have a shower in the morning?   ___

a Yes, it's beautiful here and the weather is fantastic.
b No, I don't use them a lot. I'm not really into gadgets and technology.
c I have a U2 song for phone calls and my brother singing for texts.
d Yes, and in the evening.
e Not often. About once a month, when someone has a birthday.
f At school. I take sandwiches and eat them there.
g At seven o'clock on school days but later at the weekend.

Sentence Builder Indirect object

❹ Complete the sentences using the cues and the verbs in brackets.

1 My friend / me / MP3 player for my birthday. (give)
   My friend gave me an MP3 player for my birthday.
2 I / you / email / last night. (send)
   _____
3 What questions / they / you / in the exam? (ask)
   _____
4 My mum's old school friend / her / letter last week. (write)
   _____

❺ Complete the second sentence so that it has the same meaning as the first.

1 Our teacher told a story about his family to us.
   Our teacher ___*told us a story*___ about his family.
2 You can ask the difficult questions to me.
   You can _____ questions.
3 I have never sent a text message to your dad.
   I have never _____ a text message.
4 Did you really send a letter to the Queen?
   Did you really _____ a letter?
5 Mr Green showed a film to us in history.
   Mr Green _____ in history.

❻ Read the notice and answer the questions.

Lost MP3 player

Last Friday after school, I left my MP3 player on the school bus. It is white and very small. It is an EZEE listen player.

It isn't an expensive player but I have got 300 songs on it. I haven't got the songs anywhere else – they aren't on CDs or on my computer. I don't want to lose them all.

If you find it, please give it to the bus driver or the school secretary at Edge Hill School.

Adrian Finch, Class 9B, Edge Hill School

1 Where did Adrian lose his MP3 player?
   On the school bus.
2 When did he lose it?
   _____
3 What colour is it?
   _____
4 Why is it important?
   _____
5 Who can people give it to if they find it?
   _____ or _____

❼ You lost your new digital camera at school last Wednesday. It has got lots of important photos on it. Write a 'lost' notice for the school noticeboard.

• Say where and when you lost it
• Describe it
• Say why it is important to you
• Tell people who to contact

GRAMMAR
Present Perfect questions

1 *** Match the questions (1-7) with the correct answers (a-g).**

1 Have you ever been to Venice?   _d_
2 Has your mum ever had a dog?   ___
3 Has your dad ever invented anything?   ___
4 Have your grandparents ever downloaded films? ___
5 Have I ever forgotten your birthday?   ___
6 Have we ever used our mobile phones in class? ___
7 Has this film ever been on television?   ___

a No, they haven't.
b Yes, you have.
c No, we haven't.
d Yes, I have.
e No, he hasn't.
f Yes, it has.
g No, she hasn't.

2 *** Write the answers for the questions.**

1 Have you ever used Skype?
  (✓) _Yes, I have._
2 Has your brother ever bought a computer game?
  (✓) _____.
3 Has your sister ever been on TV?
  (✗) _____.
4 Have I ever given you a birthday present?
  (✓) _____.
5 Have your parents ever sold anything online?
  (✗) _____.
6 Have we ever played this game?
  (✓) _____.
7 Has your computer ever stopped working?
  (✗) _____.

3 **** Complete the questions with the Present Perfect form of the verbs in brackets.**

1 How many emails __have you written__ (you write)?
2 What gadgets _____ (he buy)?
3 Which games _____ (you play)?
4 How much money _____ (she spend)?
5 How many photos _____ (they upload)?
6 Where _____ (she be)?
7 Why _____ (it stop) working?
8 Who _____ (Lisa invite) to her birthday party?

Grammar Alive Talking about experiences

4 ***** Use the cues to make questions and answers.**

1 **A:** win / competition?
  B: ✗ / but / brother / win / two.
  A: _Have you ever won a competition?_
  B: _No, I haven't, but my brother has won two._

2 **A:** see / The Eiffel Tower?
  B: ✗ / but / visit / Euro Disney near Paris
  A: _____
  B: _____

3 **A:** write / a blog?
  B: ✗ / but / design websites for my friends
  A: _____
  B: _____

4 **A:** work / a shop
  B: ✓ / and / work / restaurant
  A: _____
  B: _____

5 **A:** do badly / an exam
  B: ✗ / but / never / come / first in the class
  A: _____
  B: _____

6 **A:** lose / your mobile phone
  B: ✓ / and / lose / two MP3 players
  A: _____
  B: _____

Speaking Workshop 10

Talk Builder Shopping

1 Choose the correct words to complete the sentences.

1 Good morning, sir. _b_ I help you?
   a Will   **b** Can   **c** Do
2 I'm interested in this camera. Is it easy to ___ ?
   a use   **b** make   **c** take
3 Could you show me a ___ one, please?
   a best   **b** good   **c** better
4 I'd ___ this one, please.
   a want   **b** have   **c** like
5 I'm looking ___ a laptop.
   a for   **b** on   **c** to
6 How big is the ___ ?
   a remember   **b** memory   **c** brain
7 How much ___ it? £125.
   a does   **b** has   **c** is
8 This one is £200, ___ .
   a woman   **b** girl   **c** madam

2 Match the beginnings (1-8) with the correct endings (a-h).

1 Is it easy   _e_
2 This one   ___
3 Could you show   ___
4 Has it got a long   ___
5 How   ___
6 Good   ___
7 I'd   ___
8 I'm looking   ___

a much is it?
b for a laptop.
c morning, sir.
d me a cheaper one, please?
e to use?
f like this one, please.
g battery life?
h is £12.99.

3 🔊 66 Listen to the dialogue and answer the questions.

1 What does the customer want?
   An MP3 player.
2 What colours are there?
   _____
3 How much does it cost?
   _____
4 How big is the memory?
   _____
5 Is it easy to use?
   _____
6 What does the customer want to look at next?
   _____
7 Which one does the customer buy?
   _____

4 Complete the dialogue with the customer's responses (a-h) in the correct places (1-8).

A: Good morning, madam. Can I help you?
B: ¹_Yes, I'm looking for a net book._
A: This is a nice one.
B: ²_____
A: Er, wait a minute, yes. Here's a red one.
B: ³_____
A: £250
B: ⁴_____
A: Yes, 250GB which is good for a net book.
B: ⁵_____
A: Oh yes. You can use it for about six hours.
B: ⁶_____
A: Very easy.
B: ⁷_____
A: That's right, £250. Would you like to look at a cheaper one?
B: ⁸_____

a How much is it?
b And it's £250, you said?
c Is it easy to use?
d Yes, but I don't like the colour. Do you have it in red?
e Has it got a big memory?
f And what about the battery life? Is it long?
g No, that's fine. I'd like this one. It's perfect.
h Yes, I'm looking for a net book.

Exam Choice 5

Reading

1 Read the text quickly. Match the headings (a-e) with the paragraphs (1-4). There is one extra heading.

a Meeting the local people ____
b Where to go on holiday? ____
c Useful things to take ____
d Holiday activities ____
e Online research ____

BLOG

PUBLISHED 08 SEPT | READ ALL 17 COMMENTS

We have just come home after an amazing two weeks in South Africa. Now I'm back at school and it's really cold but I won't forget the best holiday of my life. I'll upload some photos soon.

1 ____

My mum and dad hate winter. They wanted to go somewhere warm in December and have a really special holiday. Mum loves animals and dad loves surfing. They surfed the net for holiday ideas but they didn't know the best place to go. ᵃ ____ I knew what to do.

2 ____

I went on the internet and looked for people's opinions about holidays. People write about everything. ᵇ ____ I soon found the perfect place. South Africa.

3 ____

We left England on 21 December. It was winter here but summer there. It was fantastic. Mum saw lions, giraffes, elephants and other animals. ᶜ ____ Once in the Atlantic Ocean and once in the Indian Ocean. And I went white water rafting on the Orange River.

4 ____

My parents were very pleased because I had a lot of gadgets with me. Dad's camera hasn't got a big memory. On the first day, he took 180 photos. ᵈ ____ On the second day, my mum borrowed my e-book reader. On the third day, she spent £5 on a phone call to my grandparents. ᵉ ____ She used my net book. Dad used my smart phone to get news about surfing and beaches in South Africa. They used my things more than I did but they didn't help me carry my bag!

2 Read the text again. Match the sentences (1-6) with the gaps in the text (a-e). There is one extra sentence.

1 I put them on my net book.
2 That's when they asked me for help.
3 They enjoyed that a lot.
4 They tell you the good things and the bad.
5 The next evening she used Skype.
6 Dad went surfing twice.

Listening

3 〔67〕 Listen to the conversation and answer the questions about Gina.

1 What has she bought online?
_____

2 How often does she check her emails?
_____

3 Does she ever download music?
_____

4 How many blogs did she finish?
_____

5 How many Facebook friends has she got?
_____

6 What does she think the best thing online is?
_____

4 **67** **Listen again. Match the people (Gina and Oliver) with the things they say. Write G (Gina) or O (Oliver).**

1 'I like buying things online. They're cheaper.' ___
2 'I've got a smart phone.' ___
3 'I only get one or two emails a day. I check them in the evening.' ___
4 'I never download music.' ___
5 'You wrote about them on your blog.' ___
6 'I'm bored with blogs.' ___
7 'They come from all over the world.' ___
8 'I talk to my grandparents on Skype every week.' ___

Speaking

5 **Put David's part of the conversation (1-7) into the correct places (a-g) in the dialogue.**

1 How big is the memory?
2 What does that mean?
3 How do you get to it from here?
4 What other features do they have?
5 How much are they?
6 Excuse me, do you know GadgetWorld?
7 Yes, I'm looking for an e-book reader.

David: ᵃ_____
Man: Yes, I do.
David: ᵇ_____
Man: Go along this street for about 200 metres, cross the road when you get to the bank and you'll see it on the right. It's next to Perfect Pizza.
David: Great. Thanks.

...

Shop assistant: Good morning, sir. Can I help you?
David: ᶜ_____
Shop assistant: We've got these.
David: ᵈ_____
Shop assistant: 2GB. You can get about 2000 books on them.
David: ᵉ_____
Shop assistant: They can play MP3s so you can get audio books.
David: ᶠ_____
Shop assistant: They are books which someone reads so you can listen to them. We also give you a free 32GB memory card so you can have more books.
David: ᵍ_____ .
Shop assistant: They are £140.
David: Oh! That's expensive. I think I'll look on the internet. Thank you.

Use of English

6 **Complete the text with the correct words.**

I ¹_____ bought a new MP3 player. It's very easy to use. ²_____ can use it! My mum has ³_____ liked gadgets but she says it's easy, too. I think she uses it when I'm at school.

It's got ⁴_____ big memory – I've got four hundred songs on it and there's a lot of room for more. My brother likes it, too. He ⁵_____ had three MP3 players and he says that mine is ⁶_____ best one he's seen. He wants to get one now.

I bought it in ⁷_____ exciting new shop in the centre of our town. It opened three weeks ago and I've ⁸_____ there six times. Every time I go I find ⁹_____ else I want! My parents have given ¹⁰_____ some money for my birthday so I think I'll buy a video game console.

7 **Complete the words with the correct letters.**

1 Spring, summer, winter and autumn are the four s _ _ s _ _ s.
2 The number of people in a country or city is the p _ p _ _ _ t _ _ _ .
3 A f _ _ _ s _ is an area with a lot of trees close together.
4 The most important city in a country is the c _ _ _ t _ _ . It is usually the biggest city but not always.
5 Digital cameras, mobile phones, MP3 players and SatNavs are all g _ _ g _ _ _ .
6 When you want to get something from the internet and put it on your mobile phone or computer, you have to d _ _ _ l _ _ d it.
7 A phone which has many features and can do things like connect to the internet is called a s _ _ r _ phone.
8 When you look at different buildings and interesting places on holiday, you are s _ g _ _ s _ _ _ n _ .

Writing

8 **You are in New York and are sending a postcard back to a friend in England. Use the information below to write a postcard between 75 and 100 words.**

- Say where you are and give your opinions about the city.
- Tell your friend what you have done.
- Tell your friend your plans for the next day.
- Say what you like most about the city.

Check Your Progress 10

❶ Online Choose the correct words to complete the sentences.

1 I don't like ___ things online.
   a sending   **b** downloading   **c** buying
2 How often do you ___ your emails?
   a upload   **b** check   **c** use
3 How can I ___ this message to my friend?
   a download   **b** send   **c** play
4 You can ___ online for one hour.
   a use   **b** upload   **c** go
5 Have you ___ my blog?
   a read   **b** used   **c** played
6 I ___ a great game from the internet.
   a sent   **b** uploaded   **c** downloaded
7 I'm not really ___ technology.
   a onto   **b** into   **c** up to

/7

❷ Gadgets Complete the sentences with the words below. There are three extra words.

> console   digital   e-book   flash   mobile
> net   player   Sat Nav   tablet   video

1 My photos are on my USB _____ drive.
2 This _____ book is smaller than my laptop and easier to carry.
3 My parents always make films of us on holiday with their _____ camera.
4 Do you like the photos I took with my new _____ camera?
5 I read a lot in the bath so this _____ reader isn't very useful for me.
6 The _____ is telling me to turn left.
7 My dad never has his _____ phone on.

/7

❸ Present Perfect Complete the sentences with the correct forms of the verbs in brackets.

1 I _____ (never have) an MP3 player.
2 My dad _____ (be) to South Africa twice.
3 Your mum _____ (not check) her emails.
4 You _____ (not upload) your photos. I'm waiting to see them.
5 The exam _____ (start) so, please stop talking.
6 Mr James _____ (not arrive) and his class are making a lot of noise.
7 I _____ (never play) rugby. Is it dangerous?
8 He _____ (lose) his phone. Have you seen it?

/8

❹ Present Perfect Questions Use the cues to make questions and answers.

1 **A:** you / send / your emails?
   B: ✓ but / not read / this message from John
   _____
   _____
2 **A:** your mum / buy / an e-book reader?
   B: ✓ but / not put / any books on it
   _____
   _____
3 **A:** you and your friends / take / any photos?
   B: ✗ / but / we make / a film
   _____
   _____
4 **A:** Sam / upload / his photos to Facebook?
   B: ✗ / but / he write / a new blog
   _____
   _____

/8

❺ Indirect objects Choose the correct words to complete the sentences.

1 I gave the phone *you/to you.*
2 Did they send *us/to us* a postcard?
3 Come on. Show *me/to me* your photos.
4 Did your teacher ask *you/to you* any questions?
5 Kerry likes you. Why don't you send a postcard *her/to her* from Italy?

/5

TOTAL SCORE */35*

Module Diary 10

❶ Look at the objectives on page 87 in the Students' Book. Choose three and evaluate your learning.

1 Now I can _____ well / quite well / with problems.
2 Now I can _____ well / quite well / with problems.
3 Now I can _____ well / quite well / with problems.

❷ Look at your results. What language areas in this module do you need to study more?

Topic Wordlist

COUNTRY AND SOCIETY

Politics
election (n)
politics (n)
parliament (n)
campaign (n)
representatives (n)
election (n)
right (n)

CULTURE

Art and Galleries
art gallery (n)
artist (n)
collection (n)
exhibition (n)
graffiti (n)
museum (n)
painting (n)

Cultural events
critic (n)
festival (n)
review (n)
show (n)
star (n)
theatre (n)

Describing films/books
amazing (adj)
boring (adj)
brilliant (adj)
compare (v)
creative (adj)
exciting (adj)
fantastic (adj)
funny (adj)
good (adj)
great (adj)
independent (adj)
interesting (adj)
realistic (adj)
story (n)

Film
action (n)
actor (n)
actress (n)
amateur (adj)
animation (n)
camera (n)
cinema (n)
comedy (n)
costume (n)
crew (n)
dialogue (n)
director (n)
documentary (n)
drama (n)
fantasy (n)
film (n)
film maker (n)
horror (n)
lighting (n)
operator (n)
original (adj)
romance (n)
romantic comedy (n)
scene (n)
science-fiction (n)
special (adj)
special effects (n)
star (v)
thriller (n)
video (n)
western romance (n)

Music
CD (n)
concert (n)
DJ (n)
group (n)
hip hop (n)
live (adj)
musical instrument (n)
musician (n)
opera house (n)
orchestra (n)
pop (n)
pop concert (n)
rock (n)
rock song (n)

FAMILY AND SOCIAL LIFE

Daily routine
start (v)
get up (v)
go to bed (v)
go to sleep (v)
wake up (v)

Leisure time
cookbook (n)
disco (n)
free (adj)
game (n)
gardening (n)
hobby (n)
night club (n)
party (n)
relaxing (adj)
rest (v)
skate park (n)
skater (n)
skating (n)
swimming pool (n)
ticket (n)
weekend (n)

Life style
regularly (adv)
ordinary (adj)
expensive (adj)
habit (n)
home-cooked (adj)
hunt (v)
collect (v)

Relationship
boyfriend (n)
anniversary (n)
boyfriend (n)
cousin (n)
family (n)
girlfriend (n)
guest (n)

FOOD

Drink
alcohol (n)
coffee (n)
cola (n)
hot chocolate (n)
juice (n)
milk (n)
tea (n)

Eating out
waiter (n)
café (n)
cafeteria (n)
menu (n)
order (v)
restaurant (n)

Fruit and vegetable
apple (n)
banana (n)
beans (n)
broccoli (n)
cabbage (n)
carrot (n)
cherry (n)
cucumber (n)
fruit (n)
kiwi (n)
lemon (n)
lettuce (n)
melon (n)
mushroom (n)
onion (n)
orange (n)
pear (n)
potato (n)
salad (n)
strawberry (n)
tomato (n)

Meals
dinner (n)
lunch (n)
picnic (n)
meal (n)
dish (n)

Meat and fish
beef (n)
chicken (n)
lamb (n)
meat (n)
pork (n)
salmon (n)
sardine (n)
tuna (n)

Sweets
biscuit (n)
cake (n)
chocolate (n)
sweet (n)

HOUSE

Description of a house
address (n)
amazing (adj)
artificial (adj)
building (n)
comfortable (adj)
concrete (adj)
dark (adj)
flat (n)
floor (n)
glass (n)
home (n)
house (n)
light (adj)
metal (n)
place (n)
private (adj)
roof (n)
space (n)
tidy (adj)
tower (n)
traditional (adj)

Furniture and equipment
armchair (n)
bath (n)
bed (n)
bookshelf (n)
carpet (n)
chair (n)
cooker (n)
cup (n)
cupboard (n)
curtain (n)
desk (n)
dishwasher (n)
door (n)
floor (n)
fridge (n)
garden (n)
hammock (n)
lamp (n)
lift (n)
light (n)
microwave (n)
mirror (n)
oven (n)
photo (n)
picture (n)
plant (n)
plate (n)
poster (n)
shower (n)
sofa (n)
stairs (n)
stereo system (n)
table (n)
toilet (n)
TV (n)
vacuum cleaner (n)
wall (n)
wardrobe (n)
washing machine (n)
window (n)

Rooms
bathroom (n)
bedroom (n)
dining room (n)
hall (n)
kitchen (n)
living room (n)
room (n)
toilet (n)

NATURAL ENVIRONMENT

Climate
autumn (n)
climate (n)
cloudy (adj)
cold (adj)
dry (adj)
foggy (adj)
hot (adj)
icy (adj)
rain (v)
rainy (adj)
snowy (adj)
spring (n)
summer (n)
sunny (adj)
temperature (n)
weather (n)
windy (adj)
winter (n)

Fauna and flora

bee (n)
bird (n)
camel (n)
crocodile (n)
elephant (n)
flower (n)
giraffe (n)
hen (n)
insect (n)
kangaroo (n)
lion (n)
lizard (n)
monkey (n)
parrot (n)
sloth (n)
tarantula (n)
turtle (n)
wild (adj)

Landscape

area (n)
amusement park (n)
beach (n)
city (n)
continent (n)
country (n)
desert (n)
feature (n)
forest (n)
lake (n)
mountain (n)
national park (n)
rainforest (n)
river (n)
town (n)
village (n)
volcano (n)

PEOPLE

Clothes

coat (n)
dinner jacket (n)
dress (n)
hat (n)
hood (n)
jacket (n)
jeans (n)
jumper (n)
sandal (n)
shirt (n)
shorts (n)
skirt (n)

top (n)
trainer (n)
trousers (n)
T-shirt (n)
warm (adj)

Person

guy (n)
adult (n)
baby (n)
boy (n)
child (n)
girl (n)
guy (n)
pensioner (n)
person (n)
teenager (n)
woman (n)

Feelings and emotions

angry (adj)
bored (adj)
comfortable (adj)
excited (adj)
favourite (adj)
happy (adj)
hungry (adj)
nervous (adj)
sad (adj)
scared (adj)
thirsty (adj)
tired (adj)
unhappy (adj)
worried (adj)

Describing people

angry (adj)
attractive (adj)
beautiful (adj)
blond (adj)
boring (adj)
busy (adj)
clever (adj)
cool (adj)
disabled (adj)
eccentric (adj)
elegant (adj)
ethnic (adj)
experienced (adj)
famous (adj)
female (adj)
fit (adj)
foreign (adj)
friendly (adj)
funny (adj)

hard-working (adj)
intelligent (adj)
kind (adj)
long (adj)
lovely (adj)
moody (adj)
nervous (adj)
old (adj)
outgoing (adj)
poor (adj)
popular (adj)
pretty (adj)
professional (adj)
rich (adj)
serious (adj)
shy (adj)
slim (adj)
strict (adj)
talkative (adj)
tall (adj)
terrible (adj)
tidy (adj)
tired (adj)
unhappy (adj)
unique (adj)
well (adj)
worried (adj)
young (adj)

SCHOOL

Lesson

book (n)
class (n)
dictionary (n)
encyclopaedia (n)
essay (n)
lesson (n)
notebook (n)
pen (n)
pencil (n)
subject (n)

School life
break (n)
demonstration (n)
head teacher (n)
homework (n)
noticeboard (n)
presentation (n)
primary school (n)
project (n)
secondary school (n)
student (n)
studies (n)
test (n)

SCIENCE AND TECHNOLOGY

Technology
automatic (adj)
battery (n)
computer (n)
computer game (n)
desktop (n)
digital camera (n)
DVD player (n)
e-book (n)
GPS (n)
hi-tech (adj)
interactive (adj)
laptop (n)
machine (n)
mobile (n)
net book (n)
program (n)
Sat Nav (n)
screen (n)
smart phone (n)
system (n)
tablet (n)
technology (n)
touch screen (n)
USB flash drive (n)
video camera (n)
video game console (n)
virtual (adj)

Using the internet
blog (n)
navigation (n)
the Net (n)
webcam (n)
website (n)

SPORT

Equipment
canoe (n)
gym (n)
medal (n)
sports centre (n)

Sportsperson
athlete (n)
player (n)
team (n)
trainer (n)

Types of sports
aerobics (n)
athletics (n)
basketball (n)
beach volleyball (n)
climbing (n)
cycling (n)
dancing (n)
exercise (n)
football (n)
gymnastics (n)
hiking (n)
hockey (n)
horse riding (n)
ice hockey (n)
judo (n)
rugby (n)
running (n)
session (n)
skiing (n)
sport (n)
surfing (n)
swimming (n)
table tennis (n)
tennis (n)
trekking (n)
volleyball (n)
watersports (n)
white-water rafting (n)
yoga (n)

TRAVELLING AND TOURISM

Means of transport
bike (n)
bus (n)
car (n)
underground (n)

Sightseeing
cathedral (n)
group (n)
guide (n)
palace (n)
sightseeing (n)
spot (n)
square (n)
tourism (n)
tourist (n)
visit (v)

Traffic
directions (n)
driving (n)
map (n)
route (n)
sign (n)
traffic (n)
tunnel (n)

WORK

Jobs
assistant (n)
bus driver (n)
chef (n)
dentist (n)
doctor (n)
engineer (n)
gardener (n)
hairdresser (n)
lawyer (n)
nurse (n)
office worker (n)
police officer (n)
psychologist (n)
scientist (n)
secretary (n)
shop assistant (n)
teacher (n)
vet (n)
waitress (n)

Health
cold (n)
healthy (adj)
hospital (n)
overweight (adj)
smoke (v)
unhealthy (adj)

SHOPPING AND SERVICES

Describing places
bad (adj)
busy (adj)
cheap (adj)
expensive (adj)
fantastic (adj)
friendly (adj)
good (adj)
local (adj)
modern (adj)
nice (adj)
noisy (adj)
old (adj)
outdoor (adj)
quiet (adj)
relaxed (adj)
small (adj)

Exam Choice Audioscripts

Man:	This is the house. Here we are in the hall and over here is the kitchen.
Woman:	Oh. It isn't blue, it's green.
Man:	Yes. A very nice green colour and white cupboards. Here is the fridge. It's very big.
Woman:	Yes, but it's very old.
Man:	Well, yes but the cooker is very modern.
Woman:	Oh yes. It's a lovely cooker. The kitchen isn't very big. There is space for a table here and … one, two, three four chairs.
Man:	Not six?
Woman:	Six? No way.
Man:	Well, let's go to the living room. It's very light.
Woman:	Yes, it is. It's a nice room. That's a nice sofa. Are there any armchairs?
Man:	Er. No. There aren't but there are some shelves here.
Woman:	Yes. Can I see the bedrooms?
Man:	Yes, of course. This is the big bedroom. There's lots of space here for a wardrobe.
Woman:	Is there a wardrobe?
Man:	No, but there is a bed.
Woman:	Is there a wardrobe in the other bedroom?
Man:	No, that room is very small. You can't have a wardrobe in there.
Woman:	Oh.
Man:	It's a nice area here. There's a school one hundred metres from here.
Woman:	I haven't got any children.
Man:	Oh.
Woman:	Is there gas and electricity?
Man:	There's electricity. The cooker and hot water use electricity. There isn't any gas.
Woman:	Oh. Gas cookers are good.

Welcome to the Big Red Bus School information line. We have three courses for English language students this year here at the Big Red Bus School, beginner, elementary and advanced. Our courses start on September 21st. There are two lessons a week, on Mondays and Thursdays. Beginners lessons start at half past three and finish at five o'clock. Elementary lessons are from quarter past five until quarter to seven and advanced lessons are from seven o'clock until half-past eight.

Lessons are £50 a month and we have twenty places for each level. For students who studied with us last year, lessons are only £40 a month. Our school is open from ten o'clock in the morning. There are three computers free for our students to use and we have a lot of English language books that our students can take home to read.

We don't have any lessons at the weekend but the school is open from ten o'clock on Saturday mornings until twelve o'clock.

Thank you for calling. We are always happy to answer your questions about our courses and the English language. You can find more information on www.bigredbusschool.co.uk

1

Rosy:	Hello, there. Where are you going?
Dana:	I'm going to the gym. I do exercise there twice a week.
Rosy:	I went to a gym last month but I didn't like it. It was full of noisy teenagers.
Dana:	You can't join this gym before you're eighteen. It's nice and quiet.
Rosy:	Really? Where is it?
Dana:	On Church Road. Why don't you come and see it?
Rosy:	Okay, great. Let's go.

2

Frank:	Hi, there. My name's Frank.
Lisa:	Hello, I'm Lisa.
Frank:	Pleased to meet you. How do you know Nigel?
Lisa:	I'm his cousin.
Frank:	Oh right. So do you live near here?
Lisa:	No. I'm from Banbury but my family are staying here this week so Nigel invited me here to his birthday party.
Frank:	I'm very glad. Hey, Lisa. Do you play tennis …?

3

Simon:	Hello. Are you new here?
David:	Yes, I am. My name's David.
Simon:	Hi, David, I'm Simon, the teacher here. So, you're interested in judo.
David:	Yes, I am. I love watching it on the TV and I saw your poster in the shopping centre.
Simon:	Great. Well, there are nine other people who come here every week so you're the tenth. Let me introduce the others to you.
David:	Oh right. Thanks. Sorry, I'm a bit nervous.
Simon:	Don't worry, there aren't any exams today!

1

Girl: I'm lucky. My mum is a great cook and she loves cooking. She likes teaching me and my brother too so I can cook quite a lot of dishes. My mum's are better but mine are okay.

2

Girl: I eat most things. I was a vegetarian for a few months last year but I love meat so I stopped. I don't like food with a lot of salt or fat in it. Oh, I know, mushrooms. I hate them. They are awful!

3

Girl: That's a difficult question. We always go on holiday to a different country and, every year, I come home and say that the food was the best in the world! Our last holiday was to Greece so now I love Greek food but I love Spanish food, too.

4

Girl: I try to eat good food and I try not to eat unhealthy snacks. If I'm hungry, I eat carrots, not sweets. But at the weekend, my mum always makes cakes and I always eat a lot. I love them.

5

Girl: Last week, my boyfriend took me to a very nice restaurant for my birthday. The food was great but the restaurant was very formal. Next year, I want to go to the Beach Restaurant. They are very friendly and the food is good. I think that's my favourite.

Oliver:	Hi Gina, what are you doing?
Gina:	Hi, Oliver. I'm shopping. On the internet. I've bought an MP3 player.
Oliver:	Why didn't you buy it in the town centre?
Gina:	I like buying things online. They're cheaper.
Oliver:	You really love your gadgets.
Gina:	I know. I've got a smart phone. I can check my emails on it. I check them about five times an hour.
Oliver:	I only get one or two emails a day. I check them in the evening.
Gina:	And I download music. That's why I want a new MP3 player.
Oliver:	I never download music. I like buying CDs. I've got them on a shelf in my bedroom.
Gina:	I know. You wrote about them on your blog.
Oliver:	Oh yes. When are you going to write a new blog?
Gina:	Never. I'm bored with blogs. I only wrote two. I started a third but didn't finish it. I put all my news on Facebook.
Oliver:	How many Facebook friends have you got?
Gina:	Four hundred and twenty-one.
Oliver:	Four hundred and twenty-one! I've got 53. You don't know four hundred and twenty-one people.
Gina:	I know but it's fun to have online friends. They come from all over the world. It's great. I love Facebook but the best thing online is Skype.
Oliver:	I know. I talk to my grandparents on Skype every week.
Gina:	and now you're talking to me …

Exam Choice Answer Key

Exam Choice 1

1 2

2 1 d 2 c,e 3 f 4 b 5 a

3 1 F 2 T 3 T 4 F 5 F 6 T

4 1 green 2 S 3 S 4 S 5 four (chairs) 6 S 7 no armchairs (none)
8 S 9 no wardrobe (none) 10 100 metres 11 electricity

5 1 How are you 2 This is 3 Pleased to meet you 4 Why don't you
5 I'm not sure 6 Let's meet 7 See you 8 Have a good time
9 And you

6 1 a 2 c 3 a 4 b 5 c 6 b

7 1 up 2 and 3 is 4 get 5 In 6 or 7 to 8 lot 9 any 10 out
11 much 12 some

8 1 There is a kitchen, a living room and three bedrooms. There isn't a
dining room. 2 There are a lot of posters on the walls in my bedroom.
3 I have got a big desk in my room. 4 There aren't any shelves in my
room. My books are on the floor. 5 It's a great place to relax.

9 Students' own answers.

Exam Choice 2

1 A 2 B 5 C 1 D 3

2 1 240 2 110 3 8 a.m.-10 p.m. 4 9 a.m.-5 p.m. 5 8 a.m.-10 p.m.
6 Closed 7 four 8 seven 9 one 10 cinema, children's play area,
(small) art gallery

3 1 Red Bus School 2 September 21st 3 Mondays 4 Thursdays
5 3.30 (half past three) 6 6.45 (quarter to seven) 7 £50
8 10.00 (10 a.m.) 9 12.00 (twelve o'clock)

4 1 Where 2 How much 3 time does (it) start 4 kind 5 remember
6 then 7 after

5 1 restaurant 2 nightclub 3 pub 4 art gallery 5 museum
6 skate park 7 outdoor market

6 1 c 2 b 3 a 4 c 5 c 6 a 7 c 8 a

7 1 d 2 f 3 b 4 e 5 g 6 c 7 a

8 Students' own answers.

Exam Choice 3

1 1 b 2 a 3 e 4 c

2 1 b 2 c 3 b 4 c

3 1 d 2 a 3 b

4 1 F 2 T 3 T 4 F 5 F 6 T

5 1 Could 2 problem 3 one 4 next 5 left 6 middle 7 one
8 front

6 1 enough 2 because 3 one 4 is 5 from 6 with 7 to 8 on

7 1 b 2 c 3 a 4 c 5 a 6 c 7 b 8 a

8 1 there 2 call 3 Send 4 like 5 but, because 6 sorry 7 Cheers

9 and 10 Students' own answers.

Exam Choice 4

1 1 c 2 a 4 b

2 1 c 3 a 4 b

3 a 3 c 1 d 4 e 5 f 2

4 1 a 2 c 3 a 4 b 5 c 6 b 7 c 8 a

5 1 a 2 c 3 b 4 b 5 a 6 b

6 1 to 2 are 3 will 4 not 5 going 6 because 7 have 8 of
9 like

7 1 Dear Sir/Madam 2 I am writing to ask for information about
3 I'd like to know 4 I would also like 5 I look forward to hearing
from you 6 Yours faithfully

8 Students' own answers.

Exam Choice 5

1 1 b 2 e 3 d 4 c

2 1 d 2 a 3 - 4 b 5 e 6 c

3 1 An MP3 player 2 (about) five times an hour 3 Yes, she does.
4 two 5 421 5 Skype

4 1 G 2 G 3 O 4 O 5 G 6 G 7 G 8 O

5 a 6 b 3 c 7 d 1 e 4 f 2 g 5

6 1 have 2 Anyone 3 never 4 a 5 has 6 the 7 an 8 been
9 something 10 me

7 1 seasons 2 population 3 forest 4 capital 5 gadgets
6 download 7 smart 8 sightseeing

8 Students' own answers.

Pearson Education Limited
Edinburgh Gate
Harlow
Essex CM20 2JE
England
and Associated Companies throughout the world.

www.pearsonELT.com

© Pearson Education Limited 2013

The right of Rod Fricker to be identified as author of this Work has
been asserted by him in accordance with the Copyright, Designs and
Patents Act 1988.

First published 2013
Seventh impression 2022

ISBN: 978-1-4479-0165-5

Set in Neo Sans Std 9pt

Printed in Slovakia by Neografia

Acknowledgements

Photo acknowledgements

The publisher would like to thank the following for their kind
permission to reproduce their photographs:

(Key: b-bottom; c-centre; l-left; r-right; t-top)

Alamy Images: Craig Joiner Photography 22, Maurice Crooks 74,
Jeff Greenberg 73, Images-Usa 5, moodboard 44, David Pearson 54,
The Print Collector 14; **Corbis:** Alex Mares-Manton / Asia Pix 87;
Fotolia.com: a4stockphotos 37, Candybox Images 12, Speedfighter
21r; **iStockphoto:** ardaguldogan 21l; **Andrew Oliver:** 9b; **Pearson
Education Ltd:** Jon Barlow 3t, Gareth Boden 65t, Jules Selmes 3b,
Banana Stock 65b; **Rex Features:** Jeff Blackler 75, Buenavist / Everett
71, Image Source 34b, Keystoneusa-Zuma 34t, OJO Images 29;
Robert Harding World Imagery: age fotostock 94; **Shutterstock.com:**
Monkey Business Images 9t; **SuperStock:** Hemis.fr 95, Image Source 17;
The Kobal Collection: Gravier Productions 46

All other images © Pearson Education

Every effort has been made to trace the copyright holders and we
apologise in advance for any unintentional omissions. We would be
pleased to insert the appropriate acknowledgement in any subsequent
edition of this publication.

Illustration acknowledgements

Illustrated by 087 Sean (KJA Artists) 8 (r), 34; John Batten 13, 45, 54,
94, 110; Andrew Painter 6, 26, 29, 68, 69, 93 (weather); Bill Piggins
12, 27, 44, 53, 55; Simon Tegg 8 (l), 16, 66, 93 (map)

Cover images: *Front:* **Alamy Images:** imagebroker l; **Corbis:** Shubroto
Chattopadhyay r; **Fotolia.com:** David Davis c, JackF cr; **SuperStock:**
Pixtal cl